I0493772

START-UP!

SO YOU WANT TO BE AN
~~ENTRPENENREUR~~
~~ENTREPENOUIR~~
~~ENTREPRENUER~~
~~ENTERPERNEUR~~

SO YOU WANT TO BE RICH!

Jim Lewis

© 2014

All rights reserved

Names and characters used herein are the product of the author's imagination or are used fictitiously. Any resemblance to any actual events or persons is purely coincidental.

Copyright © 2014 by Jim Lewis
All rights reserved. Except as permitted under the US Copyright Act of 1976, no part of this publication may be reproduced, transmitted, or distributed in any form or by any means without the prior written permission of the author.
ISBN: 1500146986
ISBN 13: 9781500146986
Library of Congress Control Number: 2014910845
CreateSpace Independent Publishing Platform
North Charleston, South Carolina

INTRODUCTION AND AUTHOR'S NOTE

Are you looking for the ultimate how-to guide to wealth and fame as an entrepreneur—you know, the kind of recipe book that you follow diligently in order to find your way to starting and running a business that will let you retire to the South Pacific in your midthirties? Well, stop reading and continue your search, because this book isn't intended to do that—mainly because most successful start-ups are the result of *not* following formulas or copying what others have done before. Just take a look at some of the people who've made it big building their own companies—Gates, Zuckerberg, Packard, Jobs, and so on; the thing that stands out most in their success is the fact that they all took different approaches to solving problems from those of the traditional thinkers in their particular fields.

The simple fact is that you won't beat the big guys by copying what they've done—you have to beat them by using their size to your advantage. Be creative, be nimble, and take risks that they are unable (due to shareholders) or unwilling (due to corporate politics) to do within their companies. The last how-to business book I read was during my MBA program thirty years ago, simply because most of those books' advice and recipes are of little value to the entrepreneur. Break the mold, challenge existing wisdom, and you just might make it big. Of course, you may also fail tragically and end up with a mountain of debt, unhappy family and friends, and no job at forty years old. But considering that you're still reading this, you just might be the kind of starry-eyed dreamer who can pull this off.

Does the fact that I don't read business books mean that I don't value education and formal learning? Absolutely not! In fact, I think that formal education is one of the key building blocks to success. I have both a BS and MBA in business as well as ten years' experience in a Fortune 500 company, all of which are vital to my success. I read constantly, including a healthy mix of fiction and nonfiction as part of my continuing education—I just happen to believe that reading books unrelated to business is far more valuable to someone running a small business than trying to learn from someone whom you'd happily put out of business.

I like to compare successful entrepreneurs to successful chefs or artists, both of whom use classical training as the foundation for building careers. Most of the celebrity chefs that you see on the Food Network (e.g., Bobby Flay or Emeril Lagasse) got their start with classical training either in schools or restaurants like the Culinary Institute or Commander's Palace, learning how to make sauces, bake pastries, and other basics of food preparation. This training (like finance or marketing classes in school) is a vital building block to success, and there are probably few (if any) people running successful restaurants who did not have some version of the basics in their backgrounds. Thousands of people go through cooking schools every year (just like business schools), so how come they don't all have cooking shows or run their own highly acclaimed restaurants around the world like Anthony Bourdain? There are two key differences between a highly successful chef and a line cook at Applebee's:

1. A different way of thinking—the line cook at Applebee's wants to make the same dish exactly the same way every time (in fact, her job depends on it) and tries to use exactly the same techniques and tools as successful chefs she has learned from. Why? Because it's safe, and doing it the same way as others who have succeeded provides a nice steady paycheck. There's nothing wrong with that, but to make it big, the entrepreneur chef views the recipes and techniques as the starting point for

creating new and different dishes that will provide a unique experiences for diners that can be built into a successful restaurant. Combining unusual ingredients in untested ways is risky (lots of awful-tasting disasters) and will likely result in getting fired from Applebee's. The successful chef takes her nose out of the cookbook and learns by listening to customers and studying trends outside the food industry.

2. Risk tolerance—a willingness to accept failure. Nobody's perfect, and anyone who tries a new recipe runs the risk of creating something that looks and tastes horrid. An entrepreneur chef is willing to deal with the occasional disaster. When someone comes up with a great new dish, it's hard not to wonder why somebody else hasn't done it before. In most cases, it probably comes down to one of three possibilities:

- Nobody else has thought of it—possible, but unlikely. At the end of the day, most likely, none of us is bright enough to have a totally unique idea or concept.
- Others have tried and discovered that it's a bad idea—it's very possible that the reason nobody puts béarnaise sauce on ice cream is because it tastes like crap.
- Other people have tried it but were unable or unwilling to make it successful—this is the most likely answer. The odds of nailing it the first time are long; and in most cases, the difference between success and failure is the willingness to stick with a good idea in spite of setbacks. The same is true in business, but more on that later.

So if this book isn't a cookbook or recipe for success, what is it? I've built and sold two successful bootstrap start-up companies, and the reason for this book is to try to help potential entrepreneurs understand key elements for success:

- Thinking creatively
- Being adaptable

- Dealing with uncertainty
- Understanding your goals and needs
- Managing your ego (your best friend and worst enemy)

One important note: this book is focused on the entrepreneur who is contemplating this adventure with a good idea but limited resources. While it will hopefully prove useful to anyone starting and running a small company, much of it doesn't apply to those who inherit a successful company or whose family provides them with resources to do it with deep pockets. I don't mean to downplay the value these people bring, and some are very successful, but the experience is very different when failure does not have any impact on your lifestyle. As a wise man once said, when you sit down for a breakfast of eggs and bacon, the chicken has an interest, but the pig is fully committed—big difference!

If you're still with me, let's get started. Hopefully we can have some fun and share some stories from my experience that will help you on your journey.

WHY DOESN'T EVERYBODY DO IT?

A few months ago I happened to catch a sound bite from a speech that President Obama gave to some group or other. In it, he addressed the owners of small businesses. I didn't get all the context of the speech, but the part I heard the leader of the free world say was, "If you have a successful business, you didn't build that." I suppose the president's message was that every small business owner benefits from investments society has made in schools, police, fire, roads, and so on, but the frustrating thing about this statement for entrepreneurs is that virtually every company out there making American products and employing American workers was started by someone with the courage to take the risk and put in the hard work to turn a great idea into a business. Whether you're talking about IBM or Apple, Amazon or Nordstrom's, the odds are that it was started and built through the efforts of individuals who felt it was worth the risk. Far too many of our politicians today have never even held "real" jobs, much less built successful companies, and this has led to policies that make realizing the American dream even more difficult than it already is. People willing to risk it all and take the plunge represent the best chance this country has for job growth, a growing economy, and innovation, and one would hope that our leaders would be praising those who try it rather than downplaying their achievements.

I'm a big fan of using analogies to make a point, and mine are generally either from some screwball comedy movie or sports. For the purposes of this discussion, let's compare building a successful start-up to success in sports. Michael Jordan grew up in North Carolina playing basketball in the playgrounds and parks provided by the government for the use of all. I can't say for sure, but I'm willing to bet that if you talked with the other kids playing with MJ, they all would have said that their dream was to one day be a star in the NBA—and why not? Fame, fortune, your own posse, and beautiful women make a pretty enticing life. Many of our leaders seem to believe that because the city provided the courts, the city is responsible for him winning multiple championships and a mantle full of MVP awards—so how come all the other kids didn't have similar success if they had the same opportunity? It's pretty safe to say that MJ becoming the greatest player of all time was some combination of genetics, environment, hard work, luck, and sacrifice.

The same answer almost certainly applies to kids who took junior high math with Steve Jobs or Bill Gates or Jeff Bezos. They had the same teachers, books, and buses, but somehow only a very small handful of people emerge from our school systems to be successful entrepreneurs. This brings us back to the question at the start of this chapter: why doesn't everybody do it? The job description is attractive enough—be your own boss, be the envy of your friends, and get rich. What's not to like? As I pointed out earlier, the real keys to success are a different way of thinking combined with a very high tolerance for risk, but let's take a closer look at some of the factors that allow an entrepreneur to be successful in business just as Jordan was in sports.

- Genetics: I realize that it sounds elitist to say that much of what we bring to our companies is inbred, but there is little question that many strengths and weaknesses that we bring to the task are out of our hands. Michael Jordan worked his butt off to be successful, but if his gene pool didn't lend itself to being six foot six with great hand-eye coordination, he never would have left his playground buddies in the dust. In the same way, some people are born with strengths that give them a leg up in the start-up world, and no amount of work is going to overcome that. The good news is that unlike the NBA, the business world doesn't have any fixed requirements; as long as you're honest about your strengths and weaknesses, you can overcome many genetic shortcomings.

- Environment: Having the right DNA is a major plus, but without spending time on the whole nature/nurture issue, the entrepreneur needs to have the right surroundings and support. I'm talking not only about your parents and upbringing, but also about having the right amount of support from your spouse, family, and friends.

- Hard work: Assuming you are fortunate enough to be born with the right DNA, you are still going to have to work your tail off to be successful. The playgrounds of New York are filled with people who have the size and athleticism of MJ (or better), but they never make it to the big time because they are unwilling to put in the hard work needed to get there. Coming out of UNC, MJ was a one-trick pony who was incredibly athletic and dazzled the crowd with high-flying dunks down the lane, but his real success in the NBA came when he spent the offseason working on jump shots and playing defense.

- Luck: No matter how smart you are or how hard you work, luck has to be on your side. MJ managed to avoid career-ending injuries, and entrepreneurs need a certain amount of good fortune to make things work. One of my greatest fears was that I would spend a lot of time and money developing a great new product only to have a giant competitor with great channels and deep pockets introduce something with similar features at the same time, and we would lose the first-mover advantage. A lot of really great buggy whip manufacturers didn't fare too well when Henry Ford and his pals put a car in every garage.

- Sacrifice: Most athletes have to make sacrifices to be successful, whether that means sacrificing pizza, desserts, family vacations, dates, or other sports. For start-up business owners, the major trade-offs are lifestyle, security, and free time. In my case, I left a ten-year career with a nice income, company car, health plan, forty-hour workweek, 401(k) plan, and job security for twice the hours, no pay, no health care, no vacations, and the very real possibility of pissing it all away for nothing. It's hard enough to explain to your kids why they won't get a vacation this year, but imagine the joy of telling them that you have to move because the bank is taking your house.

- Experience: Most potential entrepreneurs don't want to hear it, but one of the biggest keys to future success is experience in a particular field. Some people have the ability to simply walk into an industry and figure out how to make something unique and different, but in my view, your best chance comes from working in an established company and figuring out what they are doing right (and, more importantly, what they are doing wrong), as this provides a great deal of insight into how to use small size as an advantage—more on this later.

- Risk: You may have noted a recurring theme so far, and that's risk tolerance. One important note is that we're talking about accepting risk, not ignoring it. We know the risk is there; we just choose to accept it and move forward, and this is by far the biggest reason why everybody doesn't do it.

Much more on all these topics later, but by now you should be at least starting to build a mental checklist to see how well you might fit.

The good news in all of this, as pointed out earlier, is that (unlike sports) there are very few inherent limits to your opportunity to succeed in business—no height requirements or exceptional hand-eye coordination needed. Clearly, some people have some inherent advantages: high IQ, wealthy family members, a home with a high acceptance for risk-taking, or access to exceptional schools will all make things easier, but none of these is a requirement for starting a company. The biggest key to taking the plunge is a willingness to accept risk that most people frankly can't handle.

Over the years I've had countless discussions at trade shows, weddings, and cocktail parties with people who, upon finding out that I'm an entrepreneur, are quick to tell me that they have this great idea and are planning to take off on their own. In the first few years, I tended to nod and provide some words of encouragement and listen sympathetically to the stories. After twenty years of listening to countless stories, I finally realized that, at best, only a small handful of people were every going to try this. My typical response now is something along the lines of, "Great! When are you going to get started?"

Some of these discussions are held with people who clearly have no particular talent or vision for what their company would look like, what products they might build, or what particular advantages they bring that would make people line up to buy their new widget. At the end of the day, they simply want to maintain the hope that they can break free from the indentured servitude that is corporate America today and live the American dream of fame and fortune. I try to encourage them, but at the same time, I can't help but know that this is just a dream and that they won't ever do anything (or have the potential to do more). Too many people today look at the twenty-something billionaires of Silicon Valley and have unrealistic expectations that anyone can be wealthy and retired by age thirty. I've found that being frank with these folks is really pointless because, as with most dreams, the dreamer just needs to keep on dreaming.

I am much more interested in engaging people who have some background that would lead me to believe they have at least some potential to really do something. I really try to encourage these folks as, in my opinion, the world can't have enough start-ups. They provide the potential for high growth, employment, and an overall benefit to the economy. Most people in this category have at least some experience and knowledge of an industry, and in most cases they have some ideas in mind for how to proceed. If that's the case, I really try to engage them and get them to move forward with their ideas.

The conversations tend to go something like this:

"Great! When are you going to get started?"

"Um, well, I'm going to, uh, you know, start working on some things pretty soon."

"Have you built a prototype?"

"Not exactly, but I have some ideas."

"Written a business plan?"

"A what?"

"You know, that paper that describes the business: what you're going to build, how it's going to be successful financially, how much investment is needed, what sort of people you need, where the money is going to come from, and so on."

"Uh, nope."

"But you're close to getting started?"

"Absolutely! Can't wait to get going."

"So what's stopping you?"

At this point, the responses can be readily put into a few categories, all preceded by the phrase "I'm excited to get going, but I can't do it right now because…" followed by:

- "I've got to save up a little more money." News flash: you won't save enough money, and the longer you wait, the harder it is make the break. Your lifestyle goes up along with your income, and it just gets harder and harder to give it up.
- "My wife is expecting, and I can't lose my insurance." While I have very little doubt that Obamacare will fix this, even if

it does, you still will likely be working without a net for some period of time.

- "My kids are thirteen and fifteen, so I need to make sure I can pay for college." So nobody else will come up with this same brilliant idea you have in the next ten years and beat you to the punch?

- "I have stock options that vest in April, so it would be foolish for me to leave now." You have this brilliant gadget that nobody else has thought of that is going to make you millions, but you're going to wait to make sure you pick up a few thousand dollars of stock options? If you're still months away from April, it doesn't matter; if you're much closer, you should be doing things to set you up to hit the ground running when you quit on April 2.

I could go on with different variations on this theme, but by now you've probably noticed some common themes in these responses—some forces beyond your control make it impossible for you to make the move right now. All true and valid points, but one thing I've figured out is that all of these responses are just excuses for not moving forward and reflect a different perception of how big these obstacles are. The true entrepreneur is so fired up to get going that he or she either doesn't see or minimizes the potential for financial ruin (or, at the least, a major sacrifice) and charges ahead regardless.

This is what truly separates winners and losers in this game—the tolerance for and willingness to accept risks that others consider insurmountable obstacles. The world is full of reasons not to do this, starting with the statistics that tell you that less than 10 percent of start-ups survive more than a year or two; and of those that do survive infancy, most will never make the founders rich. So, am I saying that leaving a big company and doing a start-up is an irrational decision made by an otherwise intelligent individual?

Hell, yes, that's what I'm saying!

Anybody who is good at math won't have to spend a lot of time thinking about this to realize that the odds are against you, and the likelihood of success is pretty low. At this point, it's probably good to point out the difference between an irrational decision and an impulsive one. Just because I'm suggesting that you try something that most intelligent people won't doesn't mean that you should get liquored up at the company party and tell your boss to stuff it and that you're going to put him out of business. There are a lot of things that you can and should do before you take the big step, but if you find yourself dwelling on the downside risks, you'll probably never pull the trigger.

I often have people tell me that they are going to work on the new start-up without leaving the comfort of a nice paycheck, spending nights and weekends building up the business to the point where they can leave the corporate world behind and not miss a beat in lifestyle or make sacrifices. This sounds great, but I've never seen it work. There's a lot you can do to be ready, but at some point, you're probably going to have to make a clean break before your baby is ready to support you in the manner to which you're accustomed. This is particularly true if you plan to build something competitive with your present employer or make use of any company resources or customer information, as the last thing you need is a costly legal battle when you leave.

So, if you haven't given up yet and still think that you'd like to tackle the challenge, good for you! You're ready to embark on the wonderful world of start-ups—but be prepared for sleepless nights, mental anguish, financial sacrifice, and family arguments, as well as having your friends and family treat you like a pariah (and that's if everything goes well—don't even begin to think about what happens if the shit hits the fan).

But since you're not easily dissuaded and think you have what it takes, let's spend some time talking about challenges you're going to be facing in the next few months (and years) and some options for how to cope with them.

To demonstrate how this works, I'd like to introduce you to Dave Lavin. We will be following Dave's adventures as an entrepreneur through the rest of this book. Dave is a family man with a wife and two adoring children; he lives in Mesa, Arizona, and is the vice-president of operations for Hackman Refrigeration, the largest residential heating, ventilating, and air conditioning (HVAC) contractor in the Phoenix area. Dave started with the company almost ten years ago as an installer and technician and, through a lot of hard work and schedule shuffling, got his degree in electrical engineering from ASU about four years ago. Once he got his degree, the owner of the company promoted him to VP of ops, and he has worked in management ever since. Like most managers, he's made mistakes and learned a lot and has had some limited exposure to the financial side of the business. He took a lot of programming classes in college and found that he loves to tinker and write code in his spare time. A year or so ago, he came up with an idea for a new control system for residential HVAC that would be simple to use and save about 15 percent in energy consumption. He's made a very crude prototype using off-the-shelf components; it works pretty well but is big and ugly and impossible to install in somebody's house. He thinks he could make this into a viable product for sale to new homes at first and might even be able to make a version that would be cost-effective to retrofit into existing houses.

Dave enjoys his job at Hackman, but he knows that his chances for advancement fall somewhere between slim and none. Ed Hackman, the owner and founder of the company, has more money than God and treats the company like his personal ATM, so he's probably not going anywhere unless the cheeseburgers and bourbon catch up to him. Even if that happened, Dave's chances of moving up are just about nil, because last year, Ed's son and pride and joy, Rick Hackman, finally got his MBA and, after just over seven years, was done with college. Rick's graduation present was being made president of the company; so technically Dave reports to him, even though Rick has little interest or knowledge about the business. In all of Dave's time at the company, he's never seen Rick on a jobsite—unlike Ed, who loves nothing more than going out to new developments and having a beer with the developers and other contractors. Ed works longer hours than anybody else in the place, but Rick is content to show up sometime between nine and ten, spend two hours at lunch, and head for the golf course around three or so, if the weather is nice (needless to say, Rick never sees a Friday that doesn't deserve to be turned into a three-day weekend). He is a smart kid and actually not bad personally, but unfortunately he is the classic example of someone who was born on third base and thinks he hit a triple.

Dave knows he is bumping up against a DNA ceiling, and no matter how hard he works, he is only going to get incremental raises and the occasional bonus. He really dreads the day when Ed passes on and Rick is in charge. Besides, he knows that he can make this new home controller into a viable business, run things his way, and maybe even hit it big if all goes well. Dave has been telling his wife, Maggie, about how frustrating things are at the shop and how he doesn't see any future there. She trusts Dave, and he's always done well by the family, but she knows that they are financially secure and worries that with three kids and a mortgage, Dave might get frustrated and quit his job, leaving them high and dry. In fact, they had just had another variation of the usual discussion last night when he got home:

The garage door slammed, and Dave headed straight for the liquor cabinet without even taking off his jacket.

"Tough day at the office, hon?" Maggie asked in her most soothing voice.

"You have no idea…wanna hear what the little shit did today?" Dave replied while pouring himself most of a water glass full of Glenlivet.

"I assume you're referring to Rick?" she asked.

"Of course I'm *referring* to Rick, the golden child of Hackman Refrigeration. Who else could I possibly mean?"

Maggie paused for a few moments to let the first couple of swallows of Scotch settle in, hoping for an instant improvement in Dave's mood before pursuing the line of questioning that she hoped would prove therapeutic.

"I know you think he's a little spoiled, but he seems like a nice enough guy," she said.

Dave paused with the glass halfway to his lips and very deliberately set it down on the bar. "A little spoiled? *A little spoiled?*" he says, with increasing emphasis on "spoiled."

"Let me tell you what the boy wonder did today. Do you remember Juan, the driver who's been with us for eight years?"

"Is he the one I met at the company picnic whose wife has been sick?"

"Yeah. They've had a pretty tough go of it with her heart problems, but he's been really good about working as much as he can and letting me know when he can't make it. They've kind of had a double whammy, since they have a lot of medical bills and since he's hourly and has missed some time; things have been rough. Anyhow, today Juan came in and asked our office manager about an advance on his paycheck, which shouldn't have been an issue. The policy I wrote is clear—any employee can have an advance as long as they've worked the hours and they don't ask for an advance more than once every six months. Normally, Carol would have just handled it, but unfortunately Rick happened to walk by and asked what was going on."

"I think I see where this is headed," Maggie interjected.

"Trust me; it's worse than you think. This is Friday, so we had a mandatory safety meeting, and most of the field crew and office personnel were in the conference room across the hall. Little Ricky decides that this is the time assert his authority and share his wisdom in a very loud voice. I'll spare you the details, but basically Rick tells Juan that he needs to learn to be responsible with his money and not live paycheck to paycheck and depend on the company to bail him out all the time."

"Oh crap," was all she could say.

"Like the guy on the infomercial says, but wait, there's more. After berating him for being irresponsible, he tells Carol not to give him the advance and that Juan will simply have to take the money from his savings account and learn a valuable lesson about accountability!"

"You've got to be kidding! What happened?"

"I had been outside, meeting with one of our suppliers, and happened to wander in to the tail end of the conversation. I asked Rick if we could step into his office for a chat. He turned and walked away, and I nodded to Carol, which she knew meant that she should go ahead and cut the check so that part got taken care of. We went into his office, and I closed the door and explained the policy that Ed and I had put in place years ago about advances and told him that Juan was within the policy."

As Dave took another sip of his scotch, Maggie could tell there was more to the story, so she just said, "And..."

"And the princeling proceeded to tell me that his dad and I both had a soft spot for these guys, and that they needed to learn financial discipline. His exact words were, 'You guys let them work you with some sob story so that the money comes out of my pocket, while the money in their savings accounts keeps right on earning interest.' I tried to stay calm and explain that with what these guys earned, they had to work really hard just to meet the bills, and they had no savings. Even a little hiccup could put them behind, and Juan had had more than a little hiccup with his wife's health issues."

"And did that help?" asked Maggie.

"Not exactly. He sort of shook his head, like he couldn't imagine someone not having savings. But you know what his response was?"

"I'm almost afraid to ask."

"He just stood there for a moment and then spread his arms out like he was delivering enlightenment to the masses and told me, 'Well, then, the moron needs to get a job that pays more money!'—like it was such a simple solution that he couldn't believe I hadn't thought of it—and walked out."

"Surely he's not always that bad," Maggie said.

"No, he's always out of touch with normal people, but this was exceptional, and I found out later what had happened. It turns out that he was looking forward to taking his new boat out to their place on the lake, and his SUV broke down. The transmission shop called him this morning and told him that they couldn't get it fixed till next week, and he was pissed, which is why he took it out on Juan. So a few minutes later, I walked by, and he was on the phone with a car broker, giving him the specs on the new Suburban he wanted delivered by two o'clock this afternoon so he could go to the lake before it got dark. This was around nine thirty, and I'm thinking this guy is nuts! You can't just call and have a car delivered to your specifications in four and a half hours. Not only did the guy deliver it on time, but Rick just walked out of his office and told Carol to write him a check for $75,000, like it was petty cash, in front of all the office staff. Unbelievable! And this is the future of Hackman Refrigeration—and more importantly, my future."

After fifteen years of marriage, Maggie knew that there was more, so she asked, "So you want to make a change?"

"Yeah, I've had something I've been thinking about."

"Well, I know you've had offers from a lot of competitors. So you're planning to look around?" she prodded.

"Not exactly," he evaded.

"What exactly does 'not exactly' mean?"

"I'd like to try something on my own."

"You mean start your own HVAC company?"

"Not exactly…"

"What exactly does 'not exactly' mean?" she exclaimed.

After one more quick gulp of scotch, Dave stepped off the edge. "You know that controller I've been working on for the last few months?"

"Yes, what about it?"

"I think it has some real potential in the market and could be our real shot at success."

"So you're thinking of taking your idea to one of the refrigeration control companies and selling it to them?"

"Not exactly."

"Dave, I love you, but I swear to God, if you say 'not exactly' one more time, I'm going to kick you in the nuts so hard that your children will find you curled up on the floor whimpering like a six-year-old girl, and I don't think you want to go there!"

Despite being pretty sure that she wouldn't risk permanent damage to the family jewels, Dave decided he should just take the plunge. "Look, I think I can build a company that would design, manufacture, and sell EnerTrolls in the market to contractors."

"So this is the first I hear of this crazy idea, and it already has a name?"

"Well, I have been thinking about it for a while, but I didn't want to worry you."

"How thoughtful of you. You've been contemplating throwing away everything we've worked for and putting us in the poorhouse, and you didn't think I needed to be involved?"

"Come on, sweetheart, you're making it sound worse than it is. Besides, I don't think they actually have poorhouses in this day and age."

"Watch it, buster," Maggie hissed. Dave unconsciously glanced down at her right leg and decided that being a smartass was not likely to win the day or keep his nether region intact.

"I'm just saying that it's something that we should consider. The EnerTroll is actually pretty close to being functional, and this might be our best chance to make it big and have everything we've always wanted."

"Or piss everything away. Please just tell me that you didn't blow your cool and quit or get fired today."

"Don't be ridiculous. When have I ever done anything rash without talking it over with you?"

She didn't say a word; she merely tilted her head and waited for him to think about what he'd just said, which was exactly what happened. The temperature in the room seemed to drop a couple of degrees as he remembered the motorcycle under the tarp in the garage, the tattoo on his right butt cheek, and bits and pieces of a bachelor party in Vegas that culminated in a 4:00 a.m. phone call and a $2,500 wire transfer to the Clark County sheriff. "OK, OK, we've all done things we regret, but I really think this can work," he said finally.

"Look, I know you're really smart and a good engineer, but what do you know about running a company? No offense, but you can't even balance the checkbook."

"There are plenty of people who can help with the business side. I was talking to Mark, our tax guy, on the golf course last week, and he said he'd be happy to help."

"So your golfing buddies knew about this before I did?" she asked.

"Look, honey, I just wanted to let you know that I have thought a lot about this, and I've got some things lined up to help us get going."

"OK, I can tell this is something that's really important to you, but let's not dive in headfirst without a little more thought, all right? What's the next step?"

"Well, Mark says the most important thing is to build a business plan, so we can see if this makes sense and get an idea what we need to get going—and he can help with that. And even better, he's got problems with his AC, and I can get parts and installation at wholesale in exchange for some of his time, so it won't cost much. I've got my year-end bonus coming in a couple of months, and I've got a lot of vacation time saved up—"'

"Which explains why we haven't taken a vacation this year," she interjected.

"No...well, yes, but the important point is that we have some cushion if the plan looks good and we decide to go ahead."

"As long as you promise not to do anything stupid in the meantime, I'll give you the two months to put together the plan, and then *we* will decide if it's a good idea."

Despite the fact that Maggie saying "we" was not unlike the queen of England saying "We are not happy," Dave decided he'd survived this skirmish and should just move on. "That's great, sweetheart! I know you're going to be just as excited as I am in a couple of months."

We'll come back to Dave a little later, but now is probably a good time to talk about the most important thing in your life for the next few years. That's right—money, or more accurately, the scarcity of the same in times of need.

It's all about the money.

2

GENIUS

OK, I lied a little bit when I said it's all about the money, but somehow ending the previous chapter with "It's mostly about the money" just doesn't carry the same punch. I promise we'll get back to the money in a little bit, but frankly, if you don't have a good idea and a good strategy, the only relevance money has is how quickly you will piss yours away. As our focus here is success, I want to spend a little time talking about how great ideas come about.

Disclaimer: I don't have a PhD in psychology or neuroscience and have spent very little time actually reading about what makes some people creative, able to see things that others just don't. I think the term *genius* is greatly overused today, but the implications of genius regarding insights and new ways of looking at things really is the essence of what makes successful entrepreneurs successful; so for our purposes, I'm going to use the term in this discussion.

As I'm sure you've already figured out, I was a C student all through school, so my substitute for genius and brilliance was the ability to take complex issues and simplify them to the point where I could understand them. Basically, what I have tried to do is to dumb complex issues down so that I could get my arms around a problem and try to come up with a solution that's also understandable and relatively simple to implement. I know this sounds contradictory—seeking simple answers to complex problems—but over the years, I've come to believe that most really great ideas aren't the result of hours in the lab or focus groups. Rather, they are the result of someone taking a problem-solving approach that's different, simple, and elegant.

By the way, let me be absolutely clear about one thing: when I talk about an elegant solution to a problem, I don't necessarily mean a solution that's completely out of the blue. In my experience, most of the great ideas in a particular application are a compilation of concepts from a wide variety of sources that are right out there in the open for anyone to see. It just takes someone who is willing to step back from the problem and think about it differently than everybody else.

Lots of CEOs and other industry leaders talk about the importance of "paradigm shifts" and "thinking outside the box" while all the time creating structures and processes geared to killing off creativity. This approach leads to incremental change at best—the next model is going to be a little faster, a little better, a little cheaper, or what I call *incremental change*. Incremental change is hardwired into much of the corporate world. Most tech folks can relate to Moore's Law, which is basically incremental change hard-coded and quantified. For those not familiar with the story, a while back, Gordon Moore (the CEO of Intel and a true icon in the high-tech world) predicted that the capability of microprocessors would double every eighteen months. Proving Moore to be remarkably prescient, the capacity of microprocessors did in fact double every eighteen months for about five years. Gordon was cited as a genius and visionary for his ability to predict the course of technological progress years in advance, and it's hard to argue with the fact that his prediction was pretty much dead nuts on.

In my view, there are two possible reasons for Moore's almost incredible ability to forecast the future:

1. Based on his technical training and view of the world as CEO of Intel, he really was able to see the practical limitations of physics and manufacturing that would cap the ability of the high-tech world to produce chips, and he simply applied that knowledge; or

2. Because Gordon Moore was the CEO of Intel (the world's leading chip manufacturer), if he said that chips would double every eighteen months, then it must be true, and so this became the target for improvement. As long as the industry was meeting the boundaries of Moore's Law, they were successful; so it became a self-fulfilling prophecy

What we're really talking about is cause and effect. Was Moore's Law a simple prediction of an independent outcome, or was the outcome the result of the prediction? The high-tech world is driven by engineers, and engineers are like accountants—they love nothing more than quantifiable results (yes\no, right\wrong) and hate anything having to do with ambiguity or uncertainty; so if someone of Moore's stature provided a hard number to shoot for, then it must be right.

Maybe it was inevitable, but what if some crazy SOB in a lab somewhere said, "I think Gordon is probably right because we're using all silicon-based microprocessors, but I think if we built something based on carbon, we might be able to triple the output of micros overnight," and started mixing up some exotic blends of chemicals that actually worked as he hoped. I don't want to belabor the point, but it's this sort of different thinking about a problem that ultimately produces real breakthroughs.

The reason I bring up Moore's Law is not because I think it's wrong (clearly it wasn't, as it was almost dead on) but rather because it provides the opportunity to introduce what I call *nonlinear thinking*. I readily admit it's not the most exciting title, but for right now, just bear with me while I discuss what I mean by nonlinear thinking. The beauty of Moore's Law for my purposes is that if you plot a fixed incremental improvement (memory) over a fixed interval (eighteen months) for a five-year period, you get a straight line starting from the lower left and ending in the upper right corner. This is about as good a representation of a line as you could ask for; and I love visual aids, so it works great as this represents linear thinking (follow the line). Nonlinear thinking means trying to come up with a way not to just follow the line but to put a point on the map that's outside the line (hopefully well above). If successful, this approach changes the entire shape of the graph and sets a whole new course. This is what we're after—change the way customers experience your product so that others will be scrambling to keep up.

So how do you go about finding and implementing nonlinear solutions to problems in your target market?

First, think about the problem, not the solution. The problem with Moore's Law is that it really addressed the limitations of an existing solution (silicon-based chips) rather than addressing the problem (customers need more memory in a smaller package). If you're not clear on the difference between the two, go back and read this chapter again—the essential thing that separates genius (and success) from mediocrity is the ability to focus on the problem that you're trying to solve, not on how others have tried to solve it before.

For the sake of clarity, let's take a look at an example of nonlinear thinking completely outside the realm of business. In the early twentieth century, theoretical physicists around the world were faced with a major problem. The fundamental principles of gravity, planetary motion, and a bunch of other stuff developed by Sir Isaac Newton in the seventeenth century, while brilliant, were only mostly accurate. Using Newton's laws, you could pretty accurately say where a planet would be at any given time, but pretty accurately doesn't really cut it in the world of physics (or space travel, for that matter, as coming really, really close to landing on the moon isn't quite the same as "The eagle has landed"). On the other end of the scale, there were also some challenges in figuring out what held atoms together, why they didn't just fall apart, and what would happen if they did. Many brilliant minds spent countless hours (and miles of chalk) adding incremental pieces to the understanding of physics by solving little bits and making minor tweaks to existing proofs, inching ever closer to figuring things out.

In 1905, along came this guy named Albert Einstein (you may have heard of him) who came up with his theory of relativity. At this point I could say that I won't go into explaining the theory for reasons of brevity, but the reality is that I have no idea what that stuff is all about. The important point for us is that Al came up with this idea of relativity, not by solving the incremental equations faster than everybody else but by thinking about the problem differently. Basically, all the existing models treated time as a constant (logical, right, since time is the same for everyone?) and then tried to solve for where something was in space. Think back to algebra: x is a constant, and y is a variable, so solve the equation $xy = 24$ where x is 3. If you can't change x, then you have to figure what value of y solves the equation. In physics, the x was time (constant), and the y was planetary motion; so if x was constant, you had to figure out planetary motion in order to predict where a planet would be. Easy enough—except that no amount of brainpower could figure out a planetary motion model that was accurate.

Rather than bashing his head on the chalkboard, trying to arrive at a planetary motion model that worked, Einstein asked a different question: what if time isn't constant for everyone and actually depends on where you are and the direction and speed you're moving? This concept (space-time continuum, for the nerds out there) led him to develop a theory that explained planetary motion and time with almost perfect accuracy and, when combined with a similar thought process about mass and energy, led to the destruction of Hiroshima and Nagasaki along with the development of nuclear power. The important takeaway from this is not the outcome but rather the fact that Einstein is now recognized as a genius because he refused to treat all the traditional assumptions as gospel and looked at the problem like no one else had.

I highly recommend Isaacson's biography of Einstein, as it provides far more insight than I can, but there is one more critical point about what Einstein did in attacking this insurmountable problem: how he did it. Rather than starting with existing equations and building them out, he approached the issue of planetary motion (and the motion of all objects with mass) as a thought problem. He pictured one man on a train moving at thirty miles per hour and another man standing by the side of the tracks, watching the train go by. From the perspective of the man on the train, the lantern suspended from the ceiling was standing still, but to the man on the side of the tracks, it was moving at thirty miles per hour. Hence, the perception of the two men was relative to their own position and velocity. Extending this to light, he reasoned that the color of light (spectrum) varied based on whether the light was coming toward you, was stationary, or was moving away, and that the same concept could be applied to time (two different people might observe time to be different based on their relative positions and speed). Crappy explanation, but hopefully you get the point, Einstein didn't start from the same point as everybody else or take the same approach to solving the underlying problem. He simplified the problem and built an analogous model from outside of physics to arrive at a solution.

The concept of looking outside of your own field for a solution applies to a lot of other business opportunities as well. When I was starting my second company, I was looking for a new way to allow building owners to view their energy usage in a timely, cost-effective manner. At the time, owners of commercial buildings and government and educational facilities who wanted to submeter their buildings had to rely on one of the building automation companies (Honeywell, Johnson Controls, etc.) or one of the suppliers of electrical control systems (Square D, Eaton, etc.). Integrating this information into one of the control systems was very expensive, required using a limited selection of costly metering devices, and limited the use of the information gathered to the installed system. All of these factors limited the size of the market as few customers were willing to spend the money required to get the data, even though the information can be very valuable in monitoring energy usage in a large facility. Typically, the cost of these installations could be $5,000 to $10,000 per meter.

My thought was that there should be a way to allow building owners to install meters without needing costly system integration and to make the information readily available for use without costly software expenditures. It was basically a chicken and egg thing—the control companies weren't concerned with making the installations cheaper because they were making a great deal of money on the projects they did, and the market was small; and building owners didn't buy more because the cost was too high. I figured that if owners had a more cost-effective, flexible solution, the market could potentially grow substantially, particularly as the cost of energy was climbing rapidly. The problem was how to achieve this, especially as the dominant players in the market weren't interested. This meant that a whole new sales channel would have to be developed.

As no one was building anything similar in our industry, I had to come up with a new way of accomplishing the goal of cheap, flexible monitoring tools. The inspiration for what became our flagship product came to me when I was shopping for a video card for my PC. For those too young to remember the early days of PCs in the early '90s, at that time you basically bought a black box from IBM or Compaq. It was a piece of magical technology that you could not upgrade or repair (in fact, the cases were sealed to prevent tampering, and if you opened them, you voided the warranty). If you needed more performance or repair work, you had to take the PC back to a computer shop where a guy with Coke-bottle glasses and a well-worn Grateful Dead T-shirt would take it from you and return it in a week or so, along with a one-hundred-dollar invoice. You were not allowed to know how it was fixed and probably wouldn't have understood it anyway.

But back to the story: as I was standing in the video card aisle of the computer store, I got to thinking about how far things had come in just a few years. We had gone from an era of a closed system to one where I could choose from any number of video card options in a wide range of prices and install it myself. What had caused this massive shift in competition and greatly reduced the cost of getting a video card? Quite simply, it was the introduction of the concept of plug-and-play for components like video cards and hard drives—you could now buy any plug-and-play compatible device, and the PC software and hardware would recognize it, configure it, and allow you to use it without having to set interrupts or allocate memory. As long as the PC recognized what the device was, it could take care of everything for you. In large measure, this was one of the major drivers in the explosive growth of the personal computer market as it introduced competition and lowered costs.

As I pondered this phenomenon in the video card aisle, I wondered what would happen if the plug-and-play concept were applied to metering. What if a specially built PC (a data acquisition server, or DAS) could be designed to automatically recognize meters from multiple manufacturers and begin recording information with little or no involvement from a systems integrator? What if the DAS could be installed by any electrician without software skills and send the data anywhere in the world via the Internet, with no connection to a control system at all? We'll go into more detail on how this was accomplished later on, but this simple concept became the basis for a multimillion dollar company.

As you can see, this is hardly what I would call a stroke of genius. It was simply a matter of asking questions that others didn't ask and being willing to do a little nonlinear thinking in searching for solutions. For those of you who were hoping for some better story about going to a sweat lodge in Arizona or eating hallucinogenic mushrooms on a mountaintop in Tibet for product inspiration, sorry for bursting your bubble. In my defense, I did tell you earlier that the most elegant solutions are the result of simplifying the problem, looking for a situation where someone solved a similar problem, and stealing it. The hardest part of this is going against your training and experience to ask the questions that others haven't asked and being constrained by conventional wisdom. Please note that asking these questions and coming up with simple answers usually involves building products that are more complex than those available in the market today—it's much more challenging to build a product that is simple and robust than it is to build one that is complex and inflexible.

How do you clear your mind of what you know and look at a problem with a fresh approach? I usually find that alcohol helps (I'm not kidding) as it can free you of inhibitions and preconceived notions of how to do something. But it goes without saying that alcohol alone isn't the answer, or else the Irish would have invented everything worth having in the world. I have a few ground rules and things to think about that I give to my product managers when they are trying to come up with a new product:

1. Forget everything you know about how people are solving the problem today (if they're doing it right, you don't have much of a chance at beating them).
2. Put yourself in your customer's shoes and think about what would be an ideal solution. In the case of my last company, the customer would probably tell you that a perfect solution would be one that:
   - Was free
   - Installed itself
   - Could connect to any system
   - Used the web as a communication backbone; and
   - Takes complex data (kilowatts, kilowatt-hours) and converts it to useful information.
3. Build a functional specification around this ideal solution.
4. Add back in what you need to make it work. Looking at the perfect solution outlined above:
   - It probably can't be free, because most companies (other than social media) need to have revenue and product to survive—but the less expensive it is, the better.
   - It probably can't install itself, but if you can use a local electrician at $50 an hour, it is vastly preferable to a systems integrator at $250 an hour plus travel costs.
   - It probably can't connect to any system or meter (due to different software protocols), but you can start with the most popular ones to address the majority of the market and add others as you go along.

- Using the web is ideal because it means that, rather than starting from scratch, you can use off-the-shelf chips, leverage billions of lines of code written by others, and tie into existing networks.
- Converting complex data into useful information is much more challenging, but it is critical to the ultimate success of the product. As an example of how this works, because the DAS is connected to the web, it can capture instantaneous data about energy usage, which is of little value; add a time stamp and make the data useful—if you know how much energy you used at a particular time, you can relate it to activities within the building (lights turning on, air conditioners running, etc.).

Don't get bogged down in details—just understand the most important concept in arriving at elegant solutions: don't start with existing solutions and add or remove features; start with a clean slate and an ideal solution and only add in the costs and features you need. Most people can't do it, and if you can, you have a real chance to do something really different and profitable. Why can't most people do it? I think it's largely because from a very early age, we are taught that there is a "right" way to do things, a "right" way to think, and a "right" way to act. Just think about multiplication tables and the clothes you should wear and countless other societal norms that drive behavior and thinking. If you conform, you will be rewarded with good grades, good jobs, and access to the right kinds of people to hang out with. Break the rules, and you risk becoming an iconoclast (look it up) denied access to dinner parties and promotions. Although I fully support societal norms that allow us to live together (no murder, rape, robbery, etc.), I think that most of the norms in business are primarily designed to ensure that you play by the rules that others observe—but as far as I'm concerned, being a conformist entrepreneur is an oxymoron and a recipe for failure.

To summarize, what most people view as genius is simply one person looking at a problem differently than everybody else and having the balls to go forward. End of story.

For our purposes, let's assume that, like our buddy Dave, you have managed to uncover your inner Einstein and come up with a really cool idea that nobody else has (as far as you know). The good news is that you are already light-years ahead of most of the world and have broken free from years of conditioning. The bad news is that you now have to leave the happy world of dreamland and confront reality.

3

DON'T FOLLOW YOUR PASSION

We all have hobbies—you know, those things you do when you're not at work. Whatever those hobbies are (sports, photography, stamp collecting, writing software), they serve as a welcome break from the day-to-day grind of getting up every day and heading to work, slaving away so The Man can make money from our efforts. For people who find something they really love, a hobby can develop into a passion—something that we really enjoy and devote many hours to getting better at and trying to find more time to spend pursuing our passion. How many of us haven't found ourselves doing something fun and enjoyable and wishing that we could somehow turn that passion into a profession?

The idea of making a business out of a hobby is a very attractive one. What could be better than doing something you love and making money at the same time? This notion is a central theme to for many entrepreneurial "gurus" who make a fortune selling books and giving seminars that are based on "following your passion" and taking some hobby that you enjoy and turn it into a start-up. On the surface, this concept seems like a can't-miss scenario for living out your dream—do something you love and get rich doing it. The usual mantra is something along the line of "Follow your passion, and the money will come." Another appealing aspect to this idea is that it lends itself nicely to the thinking among many would-be entrepreneurs that you can take something you enjoy and just do more of it till it gets to the point of being able to support you in the manner you have become accustomed to and then just follow the path to wealth.

As with many affairs of the heart, the biggest problem with this dream scenario is that rational thinking takes a backseat to emotion. Consider for a moment the lovesick young American male who meets the love of his life at a local tavern. He wants romance so badly that he is willing to overlook the shortcomings of the new love of his life and just sees the two of them blissfully running in the surf, holding hands, and sharing a bottle of wine while the ocean spray mists them with refreshing moisture. As he sits in the bar looking deep into her eyes (or other noticeable attributes) and congratulates himself on how well he is doing with her, he fails to assess the situation objectively and ask himself why a girl who is clearly a solid eight or nine on a scale of ten would spend time with a guy who is (at best) maybe a four or five. If he were in a more rational (and sober) frame of mind, he might stop and ask a few simple questions:

1. What is it about me that makes her want to spend time with me out of all the other guys in the bar—am I especially attractive or charming?
2. Why is she (apparently) here all by herself?
3. Is she just using me to make her boyfriend jealous—and potentially have him turn up and beat the crap out of me?
4. If things go well, am I prepared for the rest of the evening? Is my apartment clean? Do I have protection?
5. What if I wake up in the morning and she's madly in love and planning our life together, and I realize that the alcohol may have clouded my judgment? Do I have an escape plan?

If this analogy seems like a stretch, consider another example from my life. One of my hobbies is photography, particularly outdoor scenes like wildlife, waterfalls, and landscapes, and I spend a great deal of time hiking into remote areas to take pictures and enjoy the scenery. I also schedule vacations around locations where I want to see and photograph new places and animals (we just finished a cruise to Southeast Asia that was focused around the Great Barrier Reef and Komodo Island, where I was able to film Komodo dragons in the wild). Mainly through trial and error, over the last twenty-nine years, I've gotten to the point where I can usually take pictures that are better than what most people would take in the same situation. I'm definitely not a "real" photographer, but I would classify myself as a pretty good amateur. I have some skills at taking the pictures and have also learned some techniques for postprocessing in Photoshop that help me correct some things that I may have screwed up in the field. I think that I really enjoy photography partly because it represents a challenge technically but mainly because it gives me an excuse to spend hours hiking the Columbia Gorge or the Indian Peaks Wilderness and seeing things that others never will.

I suspect (and my wife would certainly agree) that over the past few years, my photo hobby has crossed over into the passion scale, particularly given that I am scheduling vacations around photo opportunities and have spent several thousand dollars on new cameras, lenses, printers, and software. I've actually gotten serious enough about it to devote time to going back through the thousands of images on my computer and begin the painful process of putting my pictures into some semblance of order. Seems like a no-brainer that I should make a serious effort to follow my passion and turn to photography as a full-time job as it would not only allow me to continue doing things I enjoy but would also allow me to bring in some income to offset my expenditures on equipment and software. What could go wrong? Let's take an objective look at this plan and see what could go wrong by asking a few questions, starting from the big picture and working to more detail:

1. If I'm going to make a living at this, what unique skills or other advantages do I have over other folks who want to do the same thing? For me to get rich, I have to find people who are willing to give me money for my pictures, and that means they must be distinctive.

2. If I do find something special about my photos, is there a business model that will support me financially? The best amateur photographers in the world take great photos but don't make a dime off them.

3. Do I have the contacts I need to go to market? Unless the business model I come up with allows me to handle marketing by myself, I will probably need contacts through galleries, dealers, or magazines to sell my pictures.

4. Am I willing to adapt my dream to fit the realities of the market? No matter how much I love outdoor photography, it may turn out that the only way to support myself is taking pictures of weddings and bar mitzvahs to support my outdoor adventures.

5. Do I have the resources to carry me until this business is up and running? My current job funds the equipment, travel, and time to take pictures, but as a professional I will be competing with people who are well-established in this business and have the support of editors and others who will fund trips.

6. How much support do I have from others around me? My wife and family are very supportive of my hobby and don't object (much) to the time and money I spend pursuing it. They might not be quite as supportive when I tell them that I want to give up my six-figure income, health care, and other benefits to make this successful.

7. What happens if I fail? This is the toughest question for any would-be entrepreneur to face as it requires him or her to confront the very high potential for failure and necessitates thinking about a backup plan. Spend too much time worrying about failure, and you'll never try, but not thinking about it at all means the fall will be much more painful.

You may have picked up on a couple of common themes to these questions. The first is that there is no discussion of how passionate I am about photography, as my passion is irrelevant to the likelihood of success in this venture. Passion will drive me to work harder and be willing to devote more time, but if I don't have the requisite skills or the market won't support my vision, the level of passion is not a factor in success. The second commonality you may have noticed is that these questions necessarily force me to look at the issue objectively and take emotion out of the equation.

Let's assume, for the sake of argument, that I am somehow able to convince my wife that giving up all our security is a good idea, and she agrees to let me go forward. The next morning I walk into the office and tell my boss to shove it as I am going to pursue my passion and leave the corporate grind behind. Right about now is when the reality of what I've done begins to hit home as I have to pack up the stuff from my desk and call my wife to come and pick me up (because I have to leave my company car at the office). I sign a bunch of papers that tell me that the check they are giving me is the last one I'll ever get and that my health insurance runs out in two weeks and I will need to transfer my 401(k) account within ninety days. All of these factors will almost certainly tend to balance out the elation of being my own boss.

I launch myself into this new endeavor, and the first few days are everything I had hoped for. I sleep till eight in the morning, grab a bite to eat, and then head out for one of my favorite hikes in the Columbia Gorge to spend the day taking fantastic pictures. I even discover that it's better than I had hoped; all the poor saps who usually clog the trails on the weekend are slaving away at the office, and I have the waterfalls all to myself. My own schedule and no one to answer to, doing what I enjoy most...what could be better?

Fast forward a few weeks. I've now got a hard drive full of great pictures, and I've printed out some of the best on my fancy new Epson photo printer to take out to show to some of the gallery owners on the Oregon coast who have all the great landscapes for sale. I've also sent a bunch of samples to *National Geographic, Sunset Magazine,* and a few others. I haven't heard anything back from any of them, but my friends tell me that they're great pictures, and I'm sure it's just a matter of time. Of course, the samples I put together turned out to be a lot more expensive than I thought because I had to get them matted and framed after I talked to some people who said they wouldn't even look at unframed photos.

I've got some appointments lined up with shops on the coast (well, sort of lined up, as the ones I talked to told me that they'd be around and I could come by if I wanted to). With a mixed feeling of excitement and fear of rejection, I load up the car, grab a handful of business cards, and set out on my first sales call. I'm not too worried, as these pics are great; and I've always figured if you have a good product, there really isn't any need for fancy PowerPoints or expensive lunches—sales is the easiest job in the world, right?

I'm hauling around a dozen of my best pictures with me (total investment just under two grand), but upon arrival in Cannon Beach, I discover that the closest parking is about a block and a half from the closest of the stores I plan to visit. So, for logistical reasons, I have to cull the list to only three of my favorites to carry around. The first three shops I go to are a waste of time as the owners are not around, and the tweakers they left in charge have no authority to make any decisions. I finally get lucky on my fourth stop and find an owner who is available and willing to give me some time. I show her the three pictures, and she tells me that they are very nice photos and that they are well presented and framed (yes!), so I decide to go for the close and ask if she wants to buy them. I'm prepared for rejection (heck, I may have to go to several stores before I find a buyer), but the look I get from her is more what I would expect if I had asked if she was OK with me rolling out a sleeping bag and crashing in the store for a few days.

"First of all, like I told you, these are nice pictures."

"Um, thanks."

"You're welcome, but take a look along that back wall where all the other pictures are."

34

"OK."

"Now, tell me what is so special and different about your pictures that I should take these others down and send them back to a photographer I've worked with for years. I don't know you from Adam, and for all I know, you just bought these pictures down the street. For me to risk a long-term relationship with someone I trust, your work would have to blow me away; and even then we wouldn't do business till you could prove you owned them and could provide me with a regular supply of new material. Even if they're yours, as far as I know, they might be the only good things you've done."

"I see what you mean."

"On top of that, you need to understand how this works. I don't buy any pictures. I can't afford to tie up a bunch of my money buying pictures from anybody who walks in off the street. If you could convince me that your stuff is really different and valuable, we could maybe talk about a consignment deal."

"Consignment?" I ask.

"Sure—this is how we handle almost all the stuff like this. Basically, you provide the finished product, and I provide the space, sales staff, insurance, advertising, and so on. If the piece sells, I get twenty percent, and you get the rest."

"Well, thanks for your time and the information. Here's my card with my website in case you change your mind."

Tail firmly tucked between my legs, I proceed on down the street, only to hear the same story with minor variations at every shop I go to. Even though all of them tell me that the pictures are very nice (or maybe even a little better than what they have), they are all adamant that they aren't going to dump their existing suppliers without a really "wow" product that will move a lot more inventory and produce a lot more revenue.

Given that I have just spent a full day getting kicked in the balls, it may seem hard to believe, but things only get worse on the two-hour drive home. Facing my family with abject failure will be painful enough, but everybody knows that you just have to pick yourself up and get back in the fight. Unfortunately, I've always been pretty good at math, and even the simplest back-of-the-napkin calculation proves the flaw in my business model. Pictures similar to mine are selling for around $350, based on my informal survey of the stores I've been in, which means that even if I were successful at selling the pictures, I would only gross $280 after the consignment fee. The direct costs of printing, matting, and framing are about $150, which will leave me a gross profit of $130 if somebody buys one. Figuring in the cost of gas and food to take the pictures and get them delivered to the stores leaves around $80.

Looking at the amount of time it takes to take the pictures, print the pictures, get them matted and framed, and deliver them to the store, I would likely be making something around ten dollars an hour if all goes well—not to mention the unfortunate fact that all this investment would all be up front, and I wouldn't see a dime until something actually sold. In order to match my previous income (ignoring the fact that I would now have to pay for my own insurance and car), I would need to sell roughly six pictures per day or almost fifty a week. Extrapolating from my one day of sales experience in the field, it certainly seemed highly unlikely that I would reach that volume of sales in my lifetime. No wonder Ansel Adams spent most of his life in a tent in Yosemite Valley—he couldn't afford anything else.

Up to this point, I had managed to make a few dollars doing some photo shoots for friends and family at birthdays, graduations, and even a couple of low-budget weddings. On a per-hour basis, it probably wasn't any better than the outdoor stuff, but given that I had no experience and didn't want to overcharge, it was something promising. If I got some more experience and a few referrals, I could see how doing this kind of gig could at least put some food on the table and maybe float me long enough to get on my feet with the work I really wanted to do. Hooray, right?

Not really, because I hate doing these kinds of projects. Not only is it boring as hell, but you have to be at the beck and call of a bunch of bridezillas (and their mothers) who can never agree on anything and conform to their schedule (oddly enough, once they have a date in mind, they are surprisingly reluctant to change just because the weather's nice and you want to go to the mountains). Oh, and one other thing: if you spend a day in the mountains shooting some great scenes and return home to find out that due to some technical failure or human error you have no pictures, you can console yourself with the knowledge that the mountains will always be there and you can probably recreate the shots pretty closely. Suffice to say the same cannot be said for weddings.

Remember how this started? I was going to take a hobby I had a passion for and be able to do it full time, be my own boss, and make tons of money. Instead, what I end up with is likely a failed business, a hobby I hate, and other people telling me what to do.

Even if it's not a hobby, the same philosophy applies to any passion. Both of my companies have been involved with energy conservation, and I'm very pleased that customers using my products were able to reduce their energy costs, reduce their use of fossil fuels, and lower the amount of emissions they put into the atmosphere, but I did it to make money, not to save the whales. I've seen countless people who were passionate about the environment and became evangelists for causes like solar power or other alternative energy sources. I have learned that in most cases, their evangelism (passion) clouded their business sense. Lots of people who were passionate about solar energy in the early days and struggled to make a living found that they were left behind when the industry finally took off and they were unable to scale their businesses to meet the needs of the market.

It's perfectly OK to pursue your hobbies and passions, but remember that your passion won't necessarily translate to business success. Hobbies are things that people do for fun; and the more people who are willing to do something for free for the simple pleasure of doing it, the more difficult it is to make a living at it. After all, it's hard to be the only hooker in a town full of nymphomaniacs.

The moral of the story is this: don't try to make your passion into a business without a great deal of forethought and soul-searching. You're far better off to find a business that you're interested in and develop a passion for it than the other way around.

4

IT'S ALL ABOUT THE MONEY

Money talks; bullshit walks.

Talk's cheap; takes money to buy whiskey.

We've all heard some variant of these sayings or something pretty close, but money means everything in the early days of a start-up. If and when you run out of money, it's game over—tuck your tail between your legs and prepare to experience the sheer joy of asking your folks if it's OK for you and your family to spend a couple of years in their base-ment. Vacations, eating out, new cars, new clothes? Fuggheddaboudit. Just try to find a job at thirty-five years old when your résumé has an eighteen-month gap. Potential employers are likely to assume that you'd happily take another shot at a startup and that they might be wasting their time and money hiring you. Obviously, this is an issue to be avoided; so how much money do you need?

The short answer is more than you think. You not only have to get the costs of the business right, but you also have to remember that you have a family to support. I don't know about you, but every personal budget I've ever made for my household has proven to fall far short of reality. The car that should have three more years before major expenses blows a transmission; your perfect ten-year-old with the per-fect smile needs $2,000 in orthodontics; the roof with a twenty-year life lasts fourteen years; and on and on.

I've always been proud of (and bragged on) the fact that the business plan for my first company estimated a cash requirement of just under $250,000 before being cash flow positive, and at the end of the day, I was within $10,000 of that number. If you're thinking that I meant to say break-even instead of positive cash flow, I didn't. Big difference between breaking even on the income statement and having enough money to pay your bills. The first earns you respect and a bill from the IRS and your accountant; the second means that you actually have a viable enterprise and just might survive. You'd be surprised how many companies go out of business and owe money to the feds because there's a positive number on the income statement (much, much more on this later).

Anyway, back to the story. I nailed the money needed by the company (which should be expected as I had not only a bachelor's degree in business but also an MBA from one of the best executive MBA programs in the Pacific Northwest, achieved at no small expense to my employer at the time). I not only had the education but also several years of management mistakes under my belt, and so I had a pretty good feel for what it takes to run a business.

Where I came up short wasn't the business side of it; it was the costs of raising a family in middle class lifestyle. I'll spare the gruesome details, but let's just say that a transmission for a 1985 Mercury Topaz was apparently handcrafted by Swiss watchmakers who charged time and a half if you wanted the car back in less than a year; and apparently it rains in Oregon (who knew?), and despite their overall tolerance for precipitation, the family objected to having it in the dining room.

One other little side note: remember that line of credit that your banker all but begged you to take last year, even though you didn't need it? Try calling him now that the roof is leaking and you're a year into owning you own company. Not only will he turn you down, he probably won't even return your calls. Despite the fact that there's more equity in the house than a year ago, you can't get them to loan you a nickel because their spreadsheet says that you have to have a full-time job with a "real" company.

My wife worked for the bank for the benefits, and they still told me to pound sand when I asked for a loan on my house. If you can think of anything that you might need money for, no matter how remote, get it before you quit the corporate world. Banks love stable, rational people, and you are no longer part of that world. Once again, much more to come about banks and small business, but just know that you should arrange every nickel of credit you can line up before you step off the edge. You might be able to borrow $50,000 on September 30, but quit your job the next day, and nobody remembers your name.

Once again, I feel the need to emphasize my intended audience for this book. If you have no idea what it means to sweat about whether the mortgage payment is going to clear or whether your Visa is going to be declined during a dinner with your first (and only) customer, you should ask your private banker what all this means (or more accurately, your daddy's private banker, since he handles your trust fund). Doesn't make you a bad person, and frankly, I'm jealous, but this book is about the people who do understand the value of a dollar and have spent most of their lives since puberty figuring out how to get enough of it to make ends meet. Most trust fund babies, or TFBs (no offense), have absolutely no idea how the real world works. The good news for the rest of us is that the TFBs will find it very hard to connect with the people you will need most. If your start-up makes it through the first few months, you will need to hire engineers, bookkeepers and assembly workers, and you will have a much better understanding of what matters to them than the TFBs do.

But back to the basics: regardless of the source of your money, you need a business plan. You need to think through what it costs to get to several milestones.

- Milestone 1—you have a prototype that you can show to potential investors, customers, and employees. Doesn't have to be perfect or pretty, but it needs to show proof of concept and enough functionality that customers can see the value. More on this later, but you should already know customers who are willing to overlook cosmetics and look at how this product will benefit them. These are what we refer to as *alpha products.*

- Milestone 2—you have interest, but now you have to somehow build enough functional products for your customers to test in the field. These are beta products; they need to be rugged enough to be installed by field personnel and still provide most of the key benefits of your product, allowing your customers to see the value for themselves. This is a step beyond the one-off hand built prototypes (commonly referred to as alphas prototypes); however, moving to this phase requires not only an investment in sales and marketing but also in engineering. This is often the most expensive part of the process as you can no longer do it all yourself—you have to start spending real dollars to pay programmers, machinists, and engineers to produce something that not only works as promised but also reassures customers that you know how to build something. Remember, they want not just one device but (hopefully) thousands or millions to sell to their customers, and they are looking not just at functionality that you can build into one device. They need to know that your product can be built in volume. The cash flow burn is really starting, and everything costs more than you think, but this is a bet-the-company moment (and not the last you'll face).

- Milestone 3—your customers are raving about the beta tests, and their customers are hounding them to deliver in quantity. Great news, right? Sort of, but now you are facing one of the biggest challenges you'll see as an entrepreneur: your customers love your product but haven't paid a dime to offset the costs of moving into production quantities, so you have to figure out how to invest in tooling, testing, certifications, and everything else that a real product requires. Feel free to pop the champagne, but make sure it's cheap champagne, because you need every penny you can put your hands on.

- Milestone 4—you had enough money to build the tooling and meet the requirements for a "real" product, and your customers loved it. In fact, they loved it so much that you have to somehow figure out how to ramp up to ten times your initial production run. Once again, an upside sort of problem, but a problem nonetheless. You sent your customers invoices for their initial small orders but still haven't been paid (once again a topic that will be covered in far more detail later), and now they want a whole bunch more ASAP. Unfortunately, your vendors are not sympathetic to your receivables issue and want to have their money on much stricter terms than you are giving your customers (remember the bank loan?) because you have no clout in this channel. Oh, by the way, your employees, your landlord, and everybody else you owe money to wants to be paid *today*.

This should all be in your business plan, even if you never intend to seek outside capital, because it's crucial for you to know what you need. If you do want to get money from friends, family, or whomever, it's even more important that you can demonstrate to them that you know what you're doing and that their money is in good hands.

The details of building a business plan are beyond the scope of this book, but if you don't have the skills and experience to do it yourself, find somebody who can, as nothing is more important in the early days than knowing how much cash you need and when. The single most important piece of the business plan is the financial section; the rest is really more an outline of how you expect to reach the numbers in the plan. Most critical for figuring out just how much money you need is the pro forma income statement. If you are not familiar with income statements, this would be a great time to go online and look into what your local community college offers in the way of introductory accounting courses. I guarantee you'll be bored to tears with debits and credits, and frankly you'll never use any of this anyway, but it's important to understand the basics to read and interpret the income statement.

This will be the most valuable tool you have not only in building your plan but in mnaging your business once it's up and running.

Back to our original question: how much money is enough to get started? The answer, unfortunately, is that how much you need is very dependent on the type of business and the products you plan to build. Will you need expensive tooling or equipment? Does your product need to be fully completed to be of value (e.g., an application-specific integrated circuit), or can you make due with off-the-shelf packaging to hold the product till you get bigger? How much of what the business needs can you provide versus how much you need to spend to hire the talent you need? The good news is that a well-thought-out business plan will lead you to at least a good idea of what the cash requirements are, keeping in mind that there are only two kinds of financial plans— lucky and wrong.

The easy part of figuring out what you need to meet your personal expenses outside of the company (mortgage, car payments, braces and so on). Unless you are planning to fund your start-up with very friendly OPM (other people's money), you will be unlikely to pay yourself anything for at least a year or two. So if you make $100,000 a year now and take home around $60,000, you'll need to have at least $60,000 to $100,000 saved up to get you through the early stages till you start to get paid. Throw in another $10,000 or so to cover the health insurance you'll need, and you may just have enough to survive until the company becomes cash flow positive and can afford to pay you.

We'll spend a lot more time on OPM a little later in this chapter when we discuss potential funding sources, but a brief commentary on raising capital is in order at this point as it's critical to your business plan. If you follow the media or take courses in entrepreneurship, you'll likely find that the focus is on how to get venture capitalists (VCs) to give you millions of dollars to execute your brilliant plan. On the surface, this may seem like a great idea—not only do you not risk your own money, but you can actually pay yourself a salary and have a nice office somewhere with comfy leather chairs and the latest in electronic toys. On top of that, you'll have a ton of money to spend on hiring engineers, software developers, sales people, and so on and can really hit the ground running. Sounds great, right?

There are many reasons to not go after VC money unless you absolutely have to, which we will discuss in more detail later, but the most important issues are control and wealth. Most people start their own companies because they want to be in charge and become wealthy. What do VCs get for their millions? A majority stake in your company—meaning that they are in control and can replace you any time they want and that they will get the bulk of the money if and when the company sells (an event they control as well). One thing you'll figure out quickly: a minority shareholder in a small company has little or no influence on the direction the company takes; and unless you own more than 50 percent, you're not in charge. Remember this.

The reason this is critical is that I want you to understand that the business plan you're writing is not for potential investors, the bank, or anyone else. This is the plan as you see it and as you'd implement it if money were not an object, and the plan's purpose is to make you think through all aspects of the company, the products, the market, and competition. Some key questions your plan should address include the following:

- What is your product, and what are its advantages over existing solutions?
- Who are the customers, and how will you reach them?
- What is the competition presently, what solutions do they provide, and what are their strengths and weaknesses?
- How much can you charge for your product, and what will it cost to build (labor, materials, subcontracts, etc.)?
- How large is the market now, and what is the growth potential?
- How many products will you sell, and what kind of market share do you expect to achieve in one year, three years, or five years?

- What skills are required to make this a reality, and what do you bring to the table?
- Have you identified the people you need to recruit to meet the needs of getting a product out, and can you get them?
- Does the technology exist to build your product, or will you be breaking new ground? If so, how do you know this can be done?
- What do you see as the primary strengths, weaknesses, opportunities, and threats (SWOT) to the new company?
- What is the exit strategy?

More on all this later, but for now, just realize that it is absolutely vital that you do an honest assessment of where you are and how ready you are to take this on. It's very hard to be objective not only about your own skill set but also about how great your product is relative to the competition. You may love your idea and want it to be the next iPhone, but deluding yourself at this point will only end up costing you a great deal of time and money and will likely lead the company to fail at some point down the road. Similarly, if you overestimate your skills or your access to needed talent, you will end up spinning your wheels when the company most needs to gain traction and make progress.

Bear in mind that the answers you provide to the above questions and others in building the business plan are not an end in themselves; they are simply the means to the end, which is building a financial plan that is realistic and achievable. As the title says, it's all about the money; and the rest of the answers to these questions are simply designed to help you arrive at the best plan and to make sure that your thinking and assumptions are consistent and support the plan.

The pro forma income statement (I think it's Latin for "in the form of" or something like that) is identical to the income statements all companies use for monitoring and reporting financial performance, with the big difference being that you're yanking most of the numbers out of your rectum (also known as SWAG, or scientific wild-ass guess).

OK, if you've really done your homework, your SWAGs will be much closer to reality, but at the end of the day, you can pretty much make the numbers say whatever you want. If you're hell-bent on going into business and want to fudge the numbers to make it more attractive, you're only fooling yourself and setting yourself up for failure; so you need to rely heavily on whatever hard data you can get your hands on and make only the assumptions that you have to. For example, if you have some idea of the size of the market, and your first SWAG at volume for the new company shows that you'll have 80 percent market share in the first year, you should probably revise your numbers down to something more realistic.

How do you get the hard data that you need? Obviously, the best info you can get is if you have sales figures from your future competitors, assuming that your product is close enough to theirs that the figures have some meaning. In many cases, there are also secondary sources such as trade journals that might publish information that you can extrapolate into near real numbers. Your best bet is to get all the data you can from multiple sources and use this info to cross-check your assumptions, as it is highly unlikely that you will have real numbers that directly translate to the market potential for your product. Two separate sources are good, but three are better, and even if you can't be certain of any one piece of data, you can still use the three (or more) sources to develop a pretty good approximation of market size or at least to establish boundaries for the assumptions you make.

So let's see how this works by looking in our friend Dave Lavin. As you may recall when we last left Dave, he and She Who Must Be Obeyed had agreed on a two-month cease-fire while he built the all-important business plan that would make or break this deal in his happy home.

By Sunday morning, all the elation of getting buy-in (sort of) from Maggie had been pushed out by two straight nights of virtually no sleep with persistent nightmares full of evil numbers and spreadsheets. He'd been so focused on the technical side of building a product that he hadn't really thought about how he was supposed to run his own company. Like it or not, Maggie had been pretty much dead on with her assessment of his business skills, and he had no clue where to start on building a business plan. He could tell you the value of every capacitor in the board from memory and knew every nuance of the code he'd written, but had absolutely no idea how that translated into sales, production, or finance. Being an engineer, he had always assumed that if you built something really cool, people would simply find out about it through some Google search and start buying. He'd always thought that the sales guys were just a bunch of order-taking schmoozers and that as long as you were making great products, the numbers would take care of themselves and you'd just end up with a pile of money at the end of the month that you could use to buy expensive toys.

The most painful part was remembering how many hours he'd spent in management meetings being bored to tears when Ed and Carol went over the financials. Ed was a big believer in everyone in the company having as much information as possible, as his theory was that informed people made better decisions; so in management meetings, he'd openly shared the financials for the month and how he used that info to make changes. Unfortunately, whenever the discussion turned from technical topics to money, all Dave heard was the wah-wah trumpet noise that the kids heard in Peanuts cartoons whenever adults were talking; and he had gained virtually nothing from all that time. The only saving grace on this Sunday morning was that he was playing golf with his accountant, Mark; and if he didn't push it too much, he could probably get some pro bono advice—as long as he was willing to lose gracefully. At the very least, he was sure that Mark could set his mind at ease enough to get some sleep.

As the day unfolded, his plan for subtly getting some free advice from Mark fell apart almost immediately. They were in the cart headed to the first tee when he let Mark in on the wonderful news.

As casually as he could, Dave told Mark, "So, I had a chat with Maggie this weekend and told her that I was thinking about maybe starting a company."

"And what was her response?" Mark asked.

"She was really excited and very encouraging about the idea."

"Yeah, I'm sure. No offense, Dave, but I've known Maggie almost as long as you have, and I seriously doubt that she was wildly enthusiastic about the idea."

"Well, maybe not wildly enthusiastic, but she did say she would at least think about it."

"Did she threaten to kick you in the nuts?"

"Yeah, how'd you know?"

With a sigh, Mark simply said, "'Cause that's what Kathy threatened to do to me when I casually mentioned leaving my corporate job to set up my own accounting practice."

"Why do they do that?" Dave wondered.

"As Kathy explained it to me later, when guys come up with really stupid ideas, they are a bit like a lion chasing a lioness in heat, oblivious to everything around him. A fat gazelle with a limp could walk right by him, and he'd never know the difference. Threatening a man's most prized possessions tends to get him back on track and listening."

"Worked for me. But anyhow, the deal is that I've got two months to put together a business plan and get her to sign off, so let's get started."

"OK, Dave, this is always a little awkward, so let's get it out of the way. I know I said I'd help, and I will, but we have to set some ground rules."

"Sounds kind of formal, Mark, but OK—shoot."

"You and I are friends, and I'm happy for you that you're so excited, but we have to keep our friendship and the business separate. Otherwise, there's a good chance we could end up with a failed business relationship and a failed friendship. I've seen it before; and besides, this is how I make my living, and I have to feed my kids. So here's the deal: I'll give you some homework assignments today, and that will be the last discussion while we're playing golf. You come in to the office later this week, and we can start putting something together. If you're flexible on schedule, I can give you a discounted hourly rate, and I'm sure some of the hours will get overlooked, but this is work, and you're going to have to pay me, OK? Except, of course, for the discount for fixing the AC at my house."

"Um, sure, of course."

"Great; glad we got that cleared up. You know, sometimes it's a bit awkward when somebody thinks that just because of friendship, I will work for nothing—or that I'll just keep racking up the bills and settle for a little equity piece once it's off the ground, which is just as bad, maybe worse."

Shit! He killed Plan A and Plan B in a single swipe, Dave thought. *Apparently we'll go straight to Plan C* (which, of course, was starting to write checks that Maggie didn't sign up for). *Oh well, I suppose it won't be the last time this happens.* "OK, so what's my homework?" he asked.

"The place to start is with the size of the market, so how big is it?"

"I have no idea; how am I supposed to know that?"

"Why am I not surprised? So, here's what we need to get started: figure out what you do know for sure, and we'll build off of that. From what you've told me, this is basically a fancy thermostat, right?"

"Well, it's a lot more than that. It has some highly refined algorithms that allow the controller to learn and extract information from usage patterns that, when combined with sensors on the unit itself, can provide optimal operating parameters for a variety of—"

"Spoken like a true engineer, but let me put it differently: your device is a better replacement for a smart thermostat, right?"

"Yes, I suppose."

"And Hackman sells programmable thermostats, right?" Mark asked.

"Yes."

"And you can find out how many programmable thermostats you sold last year, right?"

"I suppose so," Dave replied.

"So that will give us some hard numbers to start with. If we know how many Hackman sold, and we know what market share Hackman has in Phoenix, and we know how big Phoenix is relative to the rest of the United States, and how big the US market is relative to the world we can come up with an estimate of the total market."

"You're screwing with me, right? We're taking one number from one company that's a fraction of the market in one city and using it to arrive at the world market size? Why don't we just ask the magic eight ball?"

"Well, there is another option—we can commission a firm I know to do the market research, and we would have data with a much better pedigree. It'll cost us—excuse me, cost you—around $10,000 and probably won't be any more accurate in the long run. They'll pay some snot-nosed intern virtually nothing to dig through outdated information and bill us two hundred dollars an hour. The information will be very credible and just as inaccurate."

"There must be something better."

"Nope. Welcome to the start-up world. How does Thursday work for you?"

And there you have it. Even in a world where the most insignificant information is available with just a few keystrokes, most business plans are written on flimsy assumptions built on outdated information with just a hint of voodoo thrown in for good measure. Why? There are actually a couple of reasons:

- First, big companies have the resources to fund accurate, timely research on product potential. Targeted research, focus groups, and massive data center capability require time and money, two things that most start-ups don't have.
- Second, most successful start-ups choose to compete in market niches that are too small for the big companies and overlooked in most research, so little hard data is available. We'll spend a lot more time on this later, but the best market for an entrepreneur is one where he or she has the chance to move in first and become established while the market is very small, build market share, and become the dominant player and grow with the market.

So not only will you be tackling a new job wearing a whole bunch of hats you've never heard of, you're going to do it based on a plan that has all the dependability and strength of used toilet paper. Get used to it—this won't be the last time you'll be covering new ground. Besides, once the numbers are on paper, they look just as good as the ones that people pay a ton of money for, and it's really up to you to make them real. If it makes you feel any better, pretty soon you're going to be projecting numbers five years in advance that are completely without basis, so these are the most reliable numbers you'll ever have.

So what are the mechanics to get the data you need? Let's assume that our friend Dave came up with the following information in his homework assignment:

- Hackman Refrigeration sold four hundred smart thermostats last year (real data—hooray!) with an average sales price of one hundred dollars.
- Hackman has about 20 percent of the Phoenix market.
- Phoenix's population is about 3 percent of the US population.
- The US population is about 10 percent of the developed countries of the world.

So the math is simple: Hackman sold 400 units, so the Phoenix market sold 2,000 units, so the US market was 66,000 units, and so the total world market was 660,000 units at $100 each, or a total market of $66 million. Voila! See, that was simple, and now we have a solid, working number for the total world market for EnerTrolls, right?

I realize that engineers and accountants reading this are already suffering mini-seizures or simply rolling on the floor laughing, but this is really how it's done. In some ways it's a little scary, but when all is said and done, this ain't like anything you've ever done and also probably not something you're going to get comfortable with. *Get over it!* Building and running a start-up company means spending most of your life outside of your comfort zone. If you're not doing things you've never done or even heard of, then you're not far enough out on the edge.

People often ask me what is the most difficult thing about doing a start-up, and for me it has always been the lack of touchstones or benchmarks. You don't really know how you're doing at any given time, largely because nobody's ever done it this way; and you just have to keep telling yourself that you're doing great, because there is no objective reference for what you are doing. If that bothers you, con-gratulations—you are a rational human being.

Is the $66 million market for smart thermostats right? Of course not! But it's probably as good as any other number, so it's a great place to start. Does that mean you base your business plan on that number alone? No, but now is when you start to validate and tweak that number by taking a slightly different approach. Let's say, for the sake of argument, that you didn't have the four hundred units that Hackman sold. How would you decide the market size? One way might be to look at your target market and get metrics from there. In Dave's case, he might assume that most of his market would come from new home sales as the cost to retrofit an existing home would be significantly higher. He could further refine his search by limiting it to new home starts that had a value greater than, say, $250,000, where the return on investment would be highest. This information is readily available. For the sake of argument, let's assume that there were a total of fifty thousand new homes with a list price of over $250,000. This would imply that the US market for smart thermostats is fifty thousand units. This is less than the 66,000 units we estimated before, but it's close enough to tell us that we're not off by an order of magnitude, and even if we adjust and use the lower number, it's still a $50 million market when we include global sales. See what we just did? We used a completely different approach and different information sources to validate the incredibly thin numbers we came up with before. As a side note, we could also assume that some of the four hundred Hackman units went to existing homes, which would actually push the $50 million much closer to our original $66 mil-lion. See, we already feel better about the numbers, right?

Another validation approach would be to look at the annual reports of one of the big publicly traded companies that makes smart thermostats. This is a little more challenging, as a market this size is really a rounding error to a multibillion-dollar international corporation, but if you spend the time to read the segment analysis for residential controls and make some assumptions about how much comes from smart thermostats, you could potentially get another point of confirmation for your numbers. If you can get in the ballpark from three different directions, you can start to feel like you are not completely off base with your numbers.

Once again, this is how it's really done, and you'd better get used to it if you want to get into this game. Most of what you have to work with, as far as market data goes, is questionable at best; and unless you want to spend a ton of money you don't have on market research, this sort of info will just have to be good enough. Most of the decisions you make going forward will be made without enough information, and you and your gut instincts will become best friends.

Why do we care about the market size? We care for several reasons:

(1) If you are going to look for outside investors, you will need to be able to convince them that the market is large enough to provide enough return on investment (ROI) for them to be interested.

(2) The overall market size will help to validate your total business (if you have to capture 90 percent market share in the first year to hit your numbers, you are in trouble).

(3) Most importantly, the overall size of the market will have a significant impact on the operational parts of your strategy and the associated resources you need to be successful.

We'll devote a lot more time to sources of funding later, so we'll leave number 1 for now and concentrate on the importance of market size in building and executing your business plan.

One of the most important uses of market size is determining who the competition might be. We can assume that Dave knows who most of the existing players are, but there may be others out there who could be interested in the market if it is large enough. It's reasonable to assume that Dave knows the existing players (e.g., Honeywell), but given a big enough market and other external factors, there may very well be new entrants to the market. In this case, if the market were larger (say, $1 billion plus), the competitive scene could change dramatically as there may be outlier companies with no active interest in the space today but may enter from a related space. As an example, a company like Google does not have a market presence in home automation, but it does have an interest in expanding its database for information about how consumers use digital tools and communications. It also has a long-established corporate dedication to energy conservation. A competitor like Google could be a very different challenge for Dave as Google's interest is not so much in the functioning of the controller as in the data that the controller could provide regarding consumer habits and preferences.

What does this mean to Dave? The potential impact of a multinational company with billions of dollars in the bank entering this market is a two-edged sword. On the one hand, Google could step in with megadollars and destroy any opportunity for a small start-up to have an impact. On the other hand, Dave could consider approaching companies like Google (or Apple or Microsoft or Amazon) about partnering in the development of the new EnerTroll. Dave uses his expertise and proprietary algorithms to build a killer controller that also gathers and communicates relevant information about its users to someone who wants it. This approach is really tough unless you have established some credibility in the marketplace, but is at least worth considering. Which is the right approach? Welcome to the start-up world—decisions you make early on about features, partners, and markets will have a huge impact on whether your new venture flourishes or dies a painful death. As usual, there's no right answer, and you don't have anywhere near enough information, but there you go.

The overall point is this: size matters, but going after too big a market can work against you as it tends to bring in larger companies with deep pockets that can ruin your day. In my view, if you hope to bootstrap your company, the ideal market has a few characteristics:

1. It's a market you know and preferably have some experience in (the more experience, the better).
2. It's a market that is big enough to provide you with the chance to build a decent-sized company ($10 to $20 million in revenue was always my personal target).
3. It's a market that's not big enough to attract the interest of the big boys (Google and most other big tech companies aren't interested unless there are billions of dollars at stake).
4. The customer needs in the market exist and are being met by other companies, but ineffectively.
5. The market shows potential for high growth, at least in your opinion.
6. There are limited barriers to entry and limited external regulations (for example, if your goal is to cure cancer, you are probably not likely to bootstrap your company, given the requirements of the FDA and others, unless your last name is Gates or Buffett).

If the market you are looking at fails any of these tests, you should very seriously consider taking that job at your father-in-law's car dealership, as you may be biting off more than you can chew. Major, major red flag time.

So let's take a look at Dave's market and see what kind of fit we have:

1. He's got years in the business: check.
2. Building a $10 million company in a few years means about 20 percent market share: check.

3. A global market of $500–$600 million looks huge, but it's noise to the big guys: check.
4. The building automation system (BAS) companies make the devices, but poorly: check.
5. Energy savings, utility incentives, saving whales: check.
6. Basically, the product just needs to meet UL listing and compatibility with existing HVAC products: check.

The smart kids in the class are probably wondering how I came up with the $10–20 million revenue number mentioned in number two, above. Much more on this later, but for now, just know that most acquisition values for small companies are based on multiples of net income (typically somewhere between eight and twelve in the industries where I've worked), and a well-run company should produce net income equal to 20 percent of revenue; so if the revenue is somewhere between $10–20 million, then net income would be $2–4 million. Given the typical earnings multiples I used, the value of this company would be between $16 and $48 million (explained in more detail later). Assuming that you control a majority interest in the company, you could expect to walk away with between $10 million and $25 million; and if you have a lifestyle that needs more than that, you should just go ask Daddy to increase your allowance and not go through the hassle of building a start-up.

I know it's taken a long time to get here, but believe it or not, we are actually making progress at answering our original question: "How much money do you need?" Market size is one piece of the answer to that question as it will tell you what sort of scale is required to compete right out of the gate, especially for the first few years. If you can answer "yes" to the above checklist (without cheating), then you may have a company that has potential for bootstrapping, and we can start seriously looking at how much you need and where you might find it.

So, how much do you need? Now it's time to put on your big boy pants (or big girl skirt, as the case may be) and decide how big your new company is going to be in five years. I know that you don't have a single customer or a single product yet, but don't let that stop you—you are the CEO of the company that nobody knows about that is going to be the dominant player in this market in ten years, so who is better qualified to come up with the numbers? You need goals to shoot at, and so do your soon-to-be employees, customers, and vendors. If you don't believe you can do it, why should they? For our purposes, let's just say that Dave can get 10 percent of the market in five years—if we assume no growth, it will be a $5 million company five years from now (or, more importantly, a company with a market value of $8–12 million). Of course, these numbers aren't "real" or even "right" in the traditional sense, but they are reasonably achievable if we come up with a good product, a good plan, and solid execution.

So now the number for five years down the road is $5 million, etched in stone and immovable (that was probably easier than you thought, wasn't it?), so let's start figuring out what it will take to get there. Five million dollars in revenue means fifty thousand units in the fifth year, or four thousand units per month. Is this reasonable? Let's work backward and see where we end up, using some assumptions based on experience:

1. Year one won't produce much (if any) revenue. That year will be spent on development and marketing with the goal of getting a handful of units into customers' hands by the end of the year.
2. Growth rates will be high (greater than double for years two to five), but growth can be deceptive due to the relative small numbers to start.

If we conservatively assume a 2x year-over-year revenue growth rate for years two and three and a 3x growth for years four and five we can arrive at the following production and sales numbers (starting from our year 5 projection and working backwards):

- Year 5—50,000 units (4,000 per month)
- Year 4—16,000 units (1,400 per month)
- Year 3—5,000 units (400 per month)
- Year 2—2,250 units (180 per month)

Lo and behold, this doesn't look so intimidating, does it? And for the computer geeks and math nerds out there, you can probably figure out that because these are average growth rates, the first month's production in year two is actually more like twenty to thirty units, or about one per day. Looking at it this way your 5 year projection not only looks doable, but actually maybe a little light. Think of it this way: if you spend a year building something really cool and can't sell more than a unit a day, you screwed up, and you should probably learn the dollar menu at McDonald's by heart because (a) that's all you can afford and (b) you'll probably be making it in a couple of weeks.

This is a valuable skill that you need to start developing right now—taking massive, overwhelming, unachievable long-term goals and breaking them down to near-term, workable tasks. Need to be a $5-million company shipping five thousand units a month in five years? Start by selling twenty per month within a year. Need to build a product with a perfect feature set in one year? Figure out what feature you can build in this week and each succeeding week, and before you know it, you'll have fifty-two really cool features in your product within a year (unless you take vacations, which you won't). Need twenty-five great employees in year four to build all the products? Start by hiring the one you need most this month and work from there. Break the impossible down to the improbable, then break it down further to the unlikely, and then break that down to the difficult, and suddenly you are faced with the doable task that you can take care of this week.

This approach now allows us to look more seriously at how much money we need to get started. The fact that we want to be able to build four thousand units a month in year five is irrelevant, and we can ignore that for now. The important thing is that we need to build a couple of units a day in year two, and Dave knows that he could build a dozen or more a day all by himself, so there is no need to look at expensive automated manufacturing equipment. Given that we don't need expensive capital equipment in manufacturing, what are the obstacles to having a workable product ready to ship to customers starting in month thirteen? This leads us to yet more questions you need to answer honestly and objectively:

1. What are the most important features to have at launch (breaking features down to must have, should have, and nice to have)?
2. What skills do I have to meet these needs (and do I have time)?
3. Do I have access to the people or companies with the skills I lack?
4. Can I get them?
5. How much do they cost?
6. Will putting more money into the equation shorten the time to market (yes, you're planning a release in twelve months, but if you could have it ready in eight, how much is that worth?)?
7. Can you make compromises (e.g., aesthetics) that will allow you to provide a fully functional product in a shorter period of time? Yes, you'd like to have that cool Euro-design housing, but if you can get a functional product on the market three months earlier using an off-the-shelf package while you're finishing the tooling, is that OK?

So far we've spent a lot of time on the value of money and conserving it, but be very cautious about noncash options at this stage. Yes, equity is cheap at this point, but it also commits you to a long-term relationship. More on this later, but for now, just realize that tossing out equity to solve near-term needs is a great deal like proposing to the girl at the bar to meet your short-term objective of a great evening. It might seem like a small price to pay at the time, but unless you're sure you want to live with her, exhaust all other options first.

Back to our friend Dave. He now can focus on what it will take to be able to build and sell a few units a day in twelve months (or less), and he has to look at what he brings to the table and what he needs to find. To deliver a finished product, he needs the following (in order of importance):

- **Software**—if this doesn't deliver, the other features are unimportant. Dave is planning to do most of this himself in terms of the back-end functioning pieces that save energy.
- **User interface**—it can't be a black box, so it needs some way for users to put in their preferences and changes and see what is going on. User interface is not Dave's specialty, so he will probably have to find someone to make this work.
- **Hardware**—Dave has a working prototype, but it won't meet UL or be buildable, so he will have to farm this out.
- Enclosure—aesthetics aren't the most important thing, but Dave can't put some ugly, clunky piece of crap on a customer's wall, no matter how well it works.
- **Marketing**—even though Dave isn't a big believer in marketing any more than voodoo, he knows that he will need collateral materials (data sheets, installation manuals, etc.) that match the quality of the product he is producing.
- **Sales**—every engineer knows that the sales department is the most underworked and overpaid department in any company, but even Dave knows that he has no idea where to start in finding customers who are willing to buy the product.
- **Finance**—at some point, finance will be a key component of the future company, but until Dave produces a product and some revenue, the finance side of the house consists of keeping track of how much money is going out every month, and he can do that himself (with help from Maggie), so this is not an issue now.
- **Regulatory**—Dave's product is low voltage, but he will have to consider things like UL (and Conformite Europeenne (CE), if he wants to sell in Europe).

So Dave has now taken a huge project (finished EnerTroll) and broken it down to seven manageable pieces that he can assign costs to.

Once again, we have taken an overwhelming task and broken it down to individual tasks that can have costs and resources assigned to it. I think it was Michelangelo who said that creating the statue of David from a piece of marble came down to simply removing all the stone that wasn't David—simple, right?

So let's break this down and assign costs to each of the tasks we need to complete to have a product ready to sell.

Software. This is the big deal that Dave thinks will make him a fortune. He has some key algorithms that can analyze usage patterns and weather conditions and provide the end user with savings of 20 percent or more per year, providing a payback of about six months on the purchase and installation of the device on average. The software is the crown jewel of the company, and if this doesn't work, the rest doesn't matter. Dave will handle all this himself, so there is no additional cost beyond the salary he won't get and his carrying cost (insurance).

User interface. Dave knows that just a few years ago, this part would have been easy—simple USB or serial port interface that Dave could have built himself—but to keep up with companies like Nest, the EnerTroll has to not only have a local interface with a touch screen but also have Wi-Fi connectivity, provide apps for both Apple and Google smartphones and tablets, and have a website for interface. Although this is less important than the functional software, it is very critical to user acceptance in the market and must be built into the product. Dave's best guess is that this will take six months to build and will cost somewhere in the neighborhood of $40,000 to $50,000 for a finished product.

Hardware. Dave has a functioning prototype, but it is based on an off-the-shelf hardware system that is not practical for designing a final product. He needs to develop a board that can be manufactured and is based on open-source software and an ARM processor that he can source from a variety of manufacturers to meet his needs, both now and in the future. The hardware design can be based on what he already has with the additional requirement to meet any certifications required. His best guess is around 120 hours of contract time at $150 per hour for a total of around $18,000 plus layout and prototyping for a total of around $20,000.

Enclosure. This one can be a little intimidating for most of us as few people have ever dealt with designing and building a customized, sexy enclosure for a product that hasn't even been designed yet. And yes, I did use the word "sexy" in a discussion about a basic product that is going to heat and cool your house—you might be amazed at just how much the look and feel of a product matters even if you are building an industrial electrical device that will be buried in an electrical box someplace and never seen again. A sleek, well-thought-out enclosure that is also highly functional makes a statement about the quality of the design on the inside and is very reassuring to customers. In Dave's case, this is also a product that will be mounted in a highly visible area of the customer's home, so the look of the unit is as important as its functionality.

We'll talk more later about where to go for specific design ideas, but for now, let's focus on the costs involved in building something that will meet the needs of the market. Building an injection molding tool for a slick, customized housing can run anywhere from $50,000 to $250,000 or more (and also takes up to a year to build) and requires you to have a final design in hand before the steel starts to fly; so both the wallet and the calendar argue against launching into this right away. Fortunately, there are some options to diving into expensive tooling that we can use for different stages of our product development.

- *Prototype:* The goal at this stage is to produce something that you can take around to potential investors, partners, and customers that will allow them to see the functionality of the unit in a somewhat finished form. This is a very limited distribution, and you will probably only need one or two prototypes to carry around and show off to these groups. There are a number of companies that make off-the-shelf molded housings in a variety of sizes and shapes. Many are well-designed and will provide a good complement to the functional parts of the product and are very inexpensive (typically less than one hundred dollars). One note: if size is a consideration for your product (as in Dave's case with the EnerTroll), make sure that you buy the smallest possible off-the-shelf case for your prototype as it makes it easier for customers to visualize how it will look.

- *Initial production runs:* Fast forward several months—you've built and shown your prototypes to rave reviews from several customers; you've made some tweaks based on the feedback you received and are ready to roll. Even better, a couple of the dealers have indicated that as soon as you have a finished product that's ready for prime time, they would be willing to buy a couple and take them out to show off to their customers. The problem is that you can't use the prototype housing, and you don't have the time or money to have a tool made, and you really want to get product in the market while customers are excited about it. The good news is that there are many machine shops out there that specialize in building custom units by milling sheets of plastic on five-axis CNC (computer numerically controlled) milling machines. The setup and programming costs are probably less than two thousand dollars for a product like Dave's and will take a relatively short time (usually a week or two), and these companies can produce near injection-molded quality parts for a couple of hundred dollars or less for each piece. Yes, two hundred dollars each is a lot more than the five dollars per unit you will pay for injection molded parts, but it's well worth it to be in the market in a matter of weeks rather than months, and you save a hundred grand or more. There are a couple of other benefits to this approach: (1) in the event you discover changes that need to be made, they are simple and inexpensive on the CNC products versus changes to a $100,000 steel injection molding tool; and (2) the programming files needed in this process are the same ones the toolmaker will need for the injection molding tools, so you save a step. Another option at this stage is to use 3D printing, in which a product is built up layer by layer. Major advantages to 3D over machining include the ability to build cavities in the model that are impossible with CNC, the ease of making changes based on experiments, and flexibility in colors and textures. It's also not cheap, but I strongly recommend that you explore this option, as 3D printing is a fast-growing industry and costs and quality are improving very rapidly.

- *Full production:* Pat yourself on the back because if you reach this stage it means that your product is well received in the market and demand is ramping up fast enough that you need to move forward on getting tooling made for your custom housings. Break out the big, big checkbook or call your rich uncle or whatever and get things rolling. The best resource at this stage is a local plastic-molding firm (web search it) as these companies can help you find a toolmaker and will generally give you a package deal in exchange for getting the business when you begin ordering molded parts in quantity.

Marketing. In the interest of full disclosure, I feel compelled to say that I have a degree in marketing from the University of Colorado. Lest you think that this affects my objectivity regarding the value of marketing, let me share a story from my personal experience. A few months after the sale of my last company, I was on a conference call with several executives from my new employer regarding the launch of a new product that we were getting ready to release. We had already discussed engineering, production, regulatory approvals, sales, and more, and my new boss asked my thoughts about the marketing plan.

My somewhat tongue-in-cheek response was that I really didn't care much, because marketing wasn't real and I felt we should spend our time on things that were tangible and actionable. About five seconds after the call ended, he called to let me know that the VP of marketing from New York had been on the call and was somewhat less than thrilled with my flippant remark, so I think that should prove my objectivity on this subject.

Only marketing people are truly passionate about marketing, but it really is important; marketing encompasses not only advertising and promotion but also critical customer facing items such as product manuals, data sheets, installation materials, and point-of-sale literature. As with the enclosure design, your marketing materials need to be professional and useful to provide customers with the assurance of the quality of your products. Painful as it is, you need to be prepared to not only spend ten thousand dollars or more on marketing work but also to devote some of your time to meeting with your marketing team to make sure that this is done right.

Sales. This is a big deal, and later we will devote a whole chapter to it, but for budget purposes, we can assume that Dave will be the sales and marketing department, so the only costs will come from visiting customers, buying lunches, and large quantities of back-slapping and ass-kissing (get used to it).

Finance. Now is the time to hire an accounting firm and pay tens of thousands of dollars to set up your chart of accounts, develop cost-of-goods-sold numbers, and…

OK, just kidding. All Dave needs to do at this point is spend five hundred dollars on a copy of QuickBooks, work out a deal with Mark to set it up, and sweet-talk Maggie into spending a couple of hours a week on data entry. This is not intended as an endorsement of QuickBooks because (1) there are several other software packages out there, and (2) they haven't paid me a dime for the plug. Just know that I built two companies up to $10 million in revenue and sold both while still using a very basic accounting package.

Regulatory. Even though the EnerTroll is a low-voltage device behind a class-2 transformer (don't worry about it; I just wanted to dazzle the engineers with my knowledge), Dave will still have to get the device approved for safety by UL for insurance purposes, which will cost anywhere from $10,000 to $15,000. He doesn't need to spend extra money on CE compliance at this point, but he does need to make sure that the design of the hardware will meet CE standards to save costly redesign later.

So what have we accomplished with all this? Dave has taken an overwhelmingly large question ("How much money do I need?") and broken it down into small enough pieces to come up with some idea of what he needs. Of course, he's wrong, because everything will cost more and take longer than he thinks, but it is at least a place to start; adjustments will be made to this part of the plan (just like every other part of the plan) as we move forward. Here's the rough number for the first year based on the information we put together above:

- Software $0
- User interface $40,000–50,000
- Hardware (board) $20,000
- Enclosure $5,000
- Marketing $10,000
- Sales $5,000
- Regulatory $10,000–15,000

So the total direct costs of getting the EnerTroll to market are $90,000 to $105,000, not counting the costs Dave will have in supporting his family. At the end of the day, he can probably expect to need at least $200,000 to $250,000 in the first year. Assuming Dave has a cool quarter million lying around and can persuade Maggie what a great idea this is, he's home free, right? Actually, no. In the bizarro world of start-ups, the cash flow (though all negative) is most clear and predictable in the time before the company is actually up and running. Most of the start-ups that fail do so because they are unable to manage cash and growth once they are actually selling real products to real customers. If that doesn't blow your mind, consider this: the most difficult early-stage company to manage is one that is wildly successful (no, I'm serious) because cash inflow is always chasing cash outflow. More on this cheery thought later, but just realize that this is the easy part.

5

WHERE TO FIND THE MONEY

Dave knows that he still has a great deal of work to do to have a real business plan, but he also knows that Maggie was really asking how much this was going to cost; and the details of the plan would only become relevant if the money worked. The money thing is really a two-part question: part one is how much you need, and part two is where you are going to get it. Since we've sort of figured out how much he needs, this is probably a very good time to discuss the pros and cons of various sources for that money.

The title of this book is *Start-Up!*, not *Introduction to Managerial Finance,* so the scope of the discussion will be limited, the opinions will be those of the author with little basis in fact or contradictory opinions, and all examples will be constructed with the sole purpose of supporting the author's opinion. *Caveat emptor*—if you want an unbiased discussion of this topic, you should seek other sources before reaching any conclusions. With that said, let's consider where you can come up with the money you need:

1. **Personal wealth (including savings and retirement):** great if you've got it
2. **Debt:** credit cards, home equity loans, etc.
3. **Friends and family:** remember that crazy uncle you've avoided at reunions?
4. **Grants and SBA loans:** big fan of paperwork?
5. **Angel investors:** more than just money

6. Venture capitalists: the default choice

The order of these options is not coincidental. Different circumstances and products will shift the options—and in some cases may dictate a single option; for example, if you are building a product that is very capital intensive (medicines or chips) and will require millions of dollars of investment, you may have no option but venture capital, as most of us don't have a few million lying around the house. The tradeoffs as you move down the list are clear—your risk goes down, but so does your control over the company so keep that in mind as you consider your choices.

Venture Capital

Let's start our discussion with one of my pet peeves regarding funding. Much of the focus and hype in the media is on multibillion dollar IPOs (initial public offerings) like Facebook, but these start-ups represent only a tiny fraction of the start-up companies getting off the ground today. In case you've forgotten, go back and read the very first paragraphs of this book—the message is that there is not a one-size-fits-all formula for entrepreneurial success, and nowhere is this more important than in funding. Not only does the media glamorize venture capital funded IPOs, but this message trickles down and manages to find its way into classrooms, seminars, and how-to books. If you take a class in entrepreneurship, you will likely find that the focus of much of the course is on how to write a business plan that will get you funded with millions of dollars from Silicon Valley VCs.

How many times have you picked up your local paper and seen the headline in the business section saying something like "Local start-up lands $10 million venture round," accompanied by a photo of a few people standing around a conference table sipping champagne and exchanging high fives? The message this conveys is that getting funding is an end in itself, when in reality funding is only a means to the end, not the endgame. And by the way, what are they celebrating?

The fact that they have given away 51 percent of their company (and 51 percent of the value when it sells) and also ceded control to other people they hardly know—yippee! T-shirts for everyone!

Again, this is not a knock on venture capital, but simply a challenge to the notion that getting VC money is the default option. Why do I encourage entrepreneurs to exhaust other options before going after venture capital? It's very important that you understand how venture capital works and go into any relationship (as with any investors), so let's look at some basics of venture capital (greatly simplified).

Venture capital companies create funds with specific investment goals and solicit investors to put money into these funds. The companies' managers then select companies to invest in that meet the fund's guidelines. For example, a VC firm might create a fund to invest in alternative energy (solar, etc.) and seek out investors who are interested in this space. An important (and often overlooked) fact is that these funds not only have a cap on investment (e.g., $50 million) but also a specific timeline for returning the investors' money (e.g., ten years). This means that the VC promises to liquidate the holdings in the fund no later than ten years from its inception and return the profits to investors. Venture capital funds are inherently risky; most VCs will invest the money in a number of companies, knowing that most will fail, a few will provide a small return, and a small fraction will be hugely successful, so it's basically a numbers game for them. For our purposes, it's important to understand the fund structure and the burden it puts on exit strategies and timing for the entrepreneur. Also bear in mind that most VCs won't look at an investment of less than $5 or $10 million, so be sure that you need a lot of cash before you start down this path.

Let's take a look at a few characteristics that founders should think about in considering venture capital:

- **Control.** One of the reasons founders start companies is because they want to control their own destinies and be able to run a company without interference. VCs are not going to simply hand you millions of dollars and passively sit back and wait to see how things go. For their investment, they get ultimate control of the company, up to and including bringing in a new CEO if they don't like how things are going. They will always tell you up front that you are the greatest thing since sliced bread, but never kid yourself about their ultimate authority if push comes to shove.

- **Getting rich.** The second reason most founders get started is because they see a start-up as the path to becoming a millionaire (billionaire?) and retire to a life of luxury, private yachts, and expensive sports cars. Bear in mind that in giving up 51 percent of the control, you are also giving up 51 percent of the value when the company sells, IPOs or whatever. Let's say that you need to clear $10 million to live the lifestyle you want after start-up. If you own 80 percent of the company, that means that you need to sell the company for roughly $20 million (after-tax yield of around $10 million for your 80 percent after expenses - yep, your hard-earned success means you get to give the government about $5 million; once again, get over it). Using our earlier earnings multiple of 10x, that means that the company needs to have a net profit of about $2 million; so if we assume a 20 percent income as a percentage of revenue, you would need to have a company with about $10 million in sales. If you've given up half the company to VCs, you now need to have a company that has twice the revenue ($20 million) for you to get the net of $10 million that you want (and they won't invest in a company that small).

- **Endgame.** I mentioned earlier how important it is for you to have clear goals in mind for your company (i.e., whether you want to do an IPO, sell to a bigger company, build a family business, or whatever). Keep in mind that VCs solely have an interest in selling the company and distributing profits to investors; they have no interest in any kind of long-term ownership, so unless their goals and timing align with yours, be prepared to have to execute on an exit strategy that is not your first choice on a schedule that you don't control.

- **Timing**. Speaking of schedules, let's take a look at why the life of the fund is so critical to the timing of the exit strategy. The VC has promised to return the money to investors ten years from the fund's inception. This date is a hard one and not subject to much flexibility, so you can expect that as you approach the end time for the fund, the VC will be looking to start the exit strategy to meet the commitments to investors. One other note—if you approach a VC that decides to invest in the company four years after the fund was started, you don't have ten years to succeed; you have six. The termination date for the fund doesn't change based on when you get funded—it's a fixed date on the calendar.

- **Portfolio companies.** We noted earlier that a venture capital fund invests in multiple companies in the same space. Using our alternative energy fund, the fund may have an investment in a company that makes solar panels and another company that makes controls and monitoring equipment for solar installations. This can be a major advantage for both companies as the VC can make introductions and facilitate the business relationship and provide both companies with ready-made markets. On the other hand, the relationship can have negative impacts as well—one company may be encouraged to sell to another at special prices and reduce profits. Even if this pressure doesn't exist, potential customers in the general market may perceive that this pressure exists or that the companies may be sharing competitive information and may be reluctant to work with them.

- **Market delusions (expand to fit).** Remember a few pages ago when we spent time putting together some highly credible numbers for market size and share? In addition to establishing parameters for total size and growth expectations, the impact of VCs can be significant (in a bad way) on the business plan. Let's say that you have estimated a 10 percent share of the $50 million market like our friend Dave. A $5 million revenue company in five years sounds pretty darn good, but if you go out to VCs for money, you have a problem. Remember the $10 million minimum that VCs want to invest? The reason for this minimum is that the amount of time they have to invest to "help" manage a company is the same, regardless of whether they invest $1 million or $10 million, so they would prefer to invest in companies that need a bigger investment for the time they will have to commit. Keeping in mind that the VC will discount your business plan by 50 percent, your $5 million company is now $2.5 million as far as the VCs are concerned, which translates to $500,000 in net income or a market value of $5 million using our earlier multiples. Is a VC likely to invest $10 million to end up with a value of $2.5 million in five years? No. VCs want to invest in companies that have the potential to get to ten times the investment or roughly $100 million in five to ten years, and you are not even close. Bottom line here is that they won't even look at your business plan. The risk here is that the entrepreneur may be tempted to tweak the market size number to get it big enough to make it of interest to VCs (in this case, some combination of market size and share would have to be inflated by probably ten times to even get in the game). Even if you are able to convince them of this, you are likely to be confronted with targets that are completely unachievable, and you will have set yourself up for failure. Of course, the counterargument to this trap is that the extra money you get from the VCs will help you to drive the market faster and gain more market share. There is some truth here, but make sure that you are at least reasonably honest with yourself when you start to yank numbers out of your butt.

- **All the money in the world.** Any entrepreneur who tries to bootstrap a start-up finds him- or herself wishing that there was a little more money available to meet bills. Cash becomes an almost all-consuming burden, so a founder who is suddenly flush with cash from a VC may do some things that start-ups should never do.

A couple of years ago there was an article in the Portland paper about a venture capital–funded start-up that was having to cut back on staff and salaries because the company was not meeting its market projections—translation: the company had minimal revenue and was burning money like there was no tomorrow. It was a multipart series, and it caught my attention because it was following the challenges that the CEO faced in making cuts necessary for the company to adapt to the realities of the marketplace. I felt a great deal of empathy through the first part of the series. The CEO talked about how difficult it was to cut staff and tell others who had been with the company from the start that their salaries would be cut by 20 percent, and I knew exactly how this poor guy felt. He felt personally responsible for the people he had brought on and hated to make these cuts. The second part of the series began with a photo of the CEO sitting on the edge of a table in the conference room where he had to give his employees for the bad news. I couldn't help but notice that the view over his shoulder was from roughly thirty stories up in a class A office building with a million-dollar view of the Willamette River, which violated one of my cardinal rules for start-ups that are not making money. The rules are simple: (1) no hardwood larger than an eight-by-ten-inch picture frame, (2) no office space higher than the second floor of any building, (3) no views nicer than the parking lot, (4) no fancy graphics and slogans pasted on the walls, and (5) no private office spaces. Once the company is making money, these rules go out the window, but until then you have no business spending money on frills. Spend it on products, sales, or production, but nothing for amenities, period. A little research showed that this company had landed an initial venture capital round four years before and had promptly moved into some pretty expensive office space downtown. This is the danger of having all money in the world—you feel like you can afford some real niceties and having loads of VC money may lead you to make bad decisions on where to spend money.

Does this mean you shouldn't look for VC money? No, but as with everything in this book, you need to keep your eyes open. Don't blindly follow the advice or example of others—do what's right for you and your company.

Personal Wealth

I know what you're thinking—if you are a typical start-up dreamer like Dave, you are likely to be in your thirties with a spouse, kids, mortgage, car payments, and so on, and the term *personal wealth* sounds like an oxymoron. Odds are you don't have a few hundred grand lying around, and you may wonder why I list personal wealth as the first choice on my list of funding sources. The short answer is that in my view, your priority right now should be maintaining control of your company; and the more outside sources you use, the less control you have. I've done one start-up with an investor and one on my own, and I can tell you that it is a whole lot easier to build a successful company on your own than it is with someone looking over your shoulder and second-guessing everything you do. As I've told people many times, the only people I've had to answer to in running my business are the IRS and my wife (not necessarily in that order), and believe me, it's hard enough to make "bet the company" decisions without having someone questioning your every move.

As discussed earlier, the tradeoff of control and risk means that increased control means increased risk. The good news is that you don't have other people to answer to; the bad news is that you put your net worth in great peril, and this is something you have to accept if you want to call the shots. Simply put, if you opt to do this yourself with whatever resources you can find on your own, you have to realize that the statistics say that a couple of years down the road, you are likely to end up mired in debt, looking for a job, and facing the prospect of working till you're eighty years old—comes with the territory. As I've said before, being an entrepreneur will beat you up physically, emotionally, and psychologically like nothing else you've ever done (and that's if things go well).

Bear in mind that personal wealth extends beyond what you have in your checking and savings accounts. You may have a 401(k) through work that you could borrow against if needed (and yes, your financial adviser will tell you that you're crazy, but they're going to tell you that anyway, so who cares). Same thing applies to IRAs or other long-term investments you may have. In a perfect world, you wouldn't tap in to any of these retirement accounts, but you are now living in an imperfect world anyway; and most everybody you know (especially your in-laws) already thinks that you've lost your mind, so all you're really doing is providing confirmation of what they already know (this is almost a public service).

We'll talk more about debt and friends and family money shortly, but this is also the time to think about some really friendly money (Hi, Mom and Dad). Some people whose emotions cloud their judgment may be willing to gift you money for the start-up with no concrete expectations for equity of payouts (right now, each of your parents can give you and your spouse $14,000 each per year with no tax consequences). Same thing goes for your spouse's parents, so you could theoretically get $56,000 a year tax-free without having to commit to giving up a share of the company—but your in-laws are probably going to save their money so they can remodel the basement they expect you to be living in shortly. My point here is simply that any money you can get your hands on without incurring debt or giving up ownership is really personal wealth that you can access—and in reality it's the best kind, because you keep control and mitigate your risk at the same time.

Debt

Do not make the same mistake I did regarding debt (trust me, there were plenty of mistakes, but for now we'll focus on this one).

Before I quit my job, I built a budget for about eighteen months that included our savings, income from my wife's two jobs, and my 401(k) from work. My backup plan (in the unlikely event that I underestimated my expenses or the time I needed to get it going) was a home equity line of credit (HELOC) that we had started for some remodeling. The HELOC was for $10,000, and the loan officer at the bank (the same bank where my wife worked) was on me every time I came in to extend it to at least $25,000 or even more, as it would be money I could draw on at any time with no paperwork or hassle. My thinking was that I would only tap into this money if I needed it, because I didn't want to pay interest on money I didn't need—and after all, I could get it any time. Same thing for a credit card we had with the bank that would provide another $5,000 in cushion. No problem, right?

Not exactly. Remember how I mentioned that my wife worked at the bank? After I pulled the trigger on my job, she put in paperwork to get insurance coverage for the family. The branch manager asked why she was getting coverage now, and she told them that she was very excited about our new company. To make a long story short, I, of course, had failed to take into account that getting a company started is much more difficult than I thought (and takes longer) and that I was getting ready to become good friends with Mr. Murphy (you know, the guy who says anything that *can* go wrong *will*). Anyhow, eighteen months into my little venture, things were getting very tight as I had exhausted not only our savings but also my retirement money—sucks, but, of course, I could just tap into the HELOC at the bank for another $25,000 or so, and that would be more than enough to carry us. I asked my wife to stop by the loan officer's desk and tell him that we were ready to extend the HELOC to the $25,000 and go ahead and borrow the full amount. Our house value had increased since we first got the HELOC, so I was thinking that it wasn't out of the question for us to get even $50,000 if need be.

She left for work a few minutes early, and I got a call shortly after that from her. I figured I probably needed to swing by and sign some paperwork, but instead she told me there was a problem, and I had to come in and meet with Brad (the loan dude). All the way in, I was thinking, *Oh great, now I have to pay for an appraisal on the house, and that will not only cost me some money but also delay things a couple of weeks, and I really could use the cash now.* I walked into the bank and saw that she was still sitting at Brad's desk with a worried look on her face. I wandered over and said hi to Brad and asked how things were going. He replied that there was a problem: since I was no longer employed, they couldn't do the HELOC. I assumed that he meant they couldn't increase it, so I told him that was OK and we would get by with just the ten grand for now. The grimace on Sandy's face told me that I really didn't get it, but she left it to Brad to tell me that not only were they not going to increase it to $25,000, they couldn't lend us *anything* on the HELOC (and, in fact, he had quietly canceled the one we had shortly after we put in for insurance).

I should point out that I was making good progress. I had a prototype built and was very close to closing a deal with an investor/ partner as I knew I didn't have the money to fund the whole thing myself at this point. I was counting on the loan money to give me some more leverage on equity, as the more I put in, the more of the company I could negotiate for. Conversely, the less money I had to contribute, the less clout I had in negotiating the split with my new partner; so not having the $25,000 plus was going to hurt a lot—and would probably cost me at least 10 to 20 percent more of the company than I had hoped for. I knew I was screwed, so I told Brad that I understood and since we were very close to closing on the funding, I was pretty sure we could squeak by with just the $5,000 on the credit card for a few weeks. The news about the HELOC had felt like somebody had crushed my left testicle, but the look on his face made me feel a twinge in the right one as well, and it was almost a formality when he told me that our credit card limit had been reduced to $500. He did tell me that he had begged to get the bank to even keep the card open at all, but it was little consolation. The moral of this story is take whatever credit you can get in cash *before* you leave your job, as nobody will even remember your name later.

Friends and Family (F&F)

Chumming. No, not the kind your grandfather does at the Elks Lodge on Saturday night, but the kind offshore fishermen do. For those not familiar with this concept, it basically boils down to tossing small chunks of fish meat and guts into the water to attract fish like tuna. The idea is that the chum will draw game fish near the boat, and they will decide to try to eat the bait that you have on the rods. Much like debt, the time to start chumming potential F&F investors is before you have made the move (family reunions and weddings are target-rich environments, as most everybody is drinking). You chum the water by letting Uncle Henry and others know that you are thinking about starting a company—make sure you don't mention needing money, and if it doesn't come across as too phony, you can even ask for advice. It's best if you preface this conversation by asking Uncle Henry not to mention this to anyone else, so he feels like he's part of a select group (and he is—you're selecting people who have money) and may start to feel like he's part of the deal. Don't mention money, but if you work it right, he may actually ask you about investing, and of course you say something along the lines of "I'm really working to solidify some parts of my business plan, so I don't know for sure; but if you're interested, I'd be happy to get back in touch when I have things finalized." Of course you know exactly how much you need, and hell, yes, you'd like him to contribute, but this is the time to play it cool and feed him a little more inside information as you go along—more chum before you set the hook.

Does this sound a little sleazy to you, like you're taking advantage of your relationship with Uncle Henry? Well, just keep in mind that if you go to outside investors like VCs for money, you're no longer the one holding the rod and staying high and dry in the boat. And by the way, I'm assuming in this example that Uncle Henry is of reasonably sound mind and in control. If he has a drool cup under his chin and is so medicated that he has no idea who you are, I am not endorsing this strategy, because that is definitely sleazy and underhanded and will likely come back to bite you in the ass somewhere down the road— karma's a bitch.

Hitting up F&F may make you a little uncomfortable, but keep in mind that these folks are by far the most likely to give you money on friendly terms. You may only have to give up a fraction of the owner-ship you would to outsiders; and if done properly, they can even feel like they are insiders getting something that others don't have access to. If you think that's not important, just look at Bernie Madoff's client list. This is not an endorsement of what Bernie did (like most others, I hope he gets an especially friendly cellmate somewhere down the road) but rather a demonstration of how much more tolerant peo-ple are if they feel they are part of something special that others are denied. And let me say one more time: target those who can afford to take the loss, and if visiting one of your potential investors involves a trip to a nursing home, you might need to check yourself.

The only downside to F&F money is that you may end up without any F&F. What you are doing is inherently risky, and it may be difficult to convey to potential friendly investors that whatever they give you may (will?) be lost. It probably won't surprise you to learn that a whole lot of F&F approached me after my first company sold to tell me how much they wanted to invest if I decided to do another one. When I started my second company, I didn't take any outside money (includ-ing F&F), and I have very little doubt that some of these folks still har-bor a grudge, thinking I'm a greedy bastard who wasn't willing to share in the rewards when we struck it big. The reason I didn't bring in inves-tors was not because I was sure of success but rather just the opposite— I knew that way too many successful entrepreneurs become enamored with reading their own press clippings and thinking that they can't fail. I was never good at statistics (except for the first class where they talked about the odds at the crap tables), but I do know that if there is a 1 percent chance of success at doing something once, the odds of doing it twice are probably worse. I know experience counts for something, but once you notch one winner, you can start to think that your poop doesn't stink like everybody else's and get yourself in real trouble. I would much rather have people a little unhappy with me for not letting them invest than have them really pissed off when I explain that it's all gone; and my only other option would be to give them back their money if it didn't work out. Not happening on my watch.

Grants and Government Loans

Major disclaimer here: I've never gotten grants or even applied for SBA or other government loans, so this section will be even more theoretical (fictional?) than the others so far. Why haven't I taken advantage of these resources, especially given that the money they provide may be free or very cheap? When you run your own company, you quickly learn that the people you work with, whether investors, employees, partners, or vendors, are all critical to your success; and you can't afford to risk taking on investors whose goals aren't in line with yours.. Bringing on investors is very much like getting married or pregnant—surprisingly easy to get started but very challenging to undo later. When looking at investors of any kind, you need to be looking for several key things, and you should ask yourself some questions:

1. Is this a person or entity you respect?
2. Is this someone you can trust?
3. Does he or she bring something more than just money to the table?
4. Do you share common values and goals?
5. Is the person committed to the long term, and does he or she understand the challenges that small companies face?

In all my years of experience with government entities, I have only run into a few that meet any of these criteria (much less all of them); and it has always seemed to me that the amount of time and bullshit required to get your hands on this "cheap" money is simply not worth the effort. On the other hand, I have worked with a number of companies who have figured out how to make this work and have managed to build very successful businesses on government money of one kind or another, so if you want to take a shot, have at it. Remember, there is no "right" way to do this, and you should follow your own instincts, not mine.

Another avenue to consider is nongovernment grants and other support that might fit well into your business plan without all the headaches of working with bureaucrats. Companies like Google and others have established incubators and set aside funding to support start-ups building products that complement theirs, with the goal of growing their own primary business. It's probably worth taking the time to explore major players in your chosen field who might have these sorts of programs available. There are at least two reasons these may be more useful than government programs: (1) these companies understand making money and will likely have less bureaucracy; and (2) what seems like a fortune to you is just walking-around money for them, and you may be able to fly under the radar with less accountability and oversight. Probably worth a look at least.

Angel Investors

Angel investors are basically investors who will do early-stage funding of companies that are just getting going. The big advantage to angels over VCs is that the angels are typically investing their own money, so they will make much smaller investments in more risky ventures as they do not have to answer to fund investors with fixed timelines. Many of these angels have done start-ups themselves and are much more likely to understand the challenges of doing a start-up; they may bring valuable experience and connections in addition to money.

The biggest drawback to angels (like all outside investors) is that you will have to give up a piece of your company, but with angels the investment amount is far less than VCs, and so is the demand for equity and control. Most of these folks are retired and are doing this because they want to get some return on investment—but also because they really enjoy being "in the game" without having to do it themselves. For many, it's a way to "pay it forward" and provide a valuable service to the community while making some money. Be aware, however, that you do run the risk of hooking up with a retired entrepreneur who may want a more active role than you would like, so just make sure that you know what you are getting into.

In ancient times (the 1990s), finding angel investors was mostly word of mouth and a lot of gas and shoe leather, because there were few if any resources or forums to bring entrepreneurs and investors together. Today almost every city has one or more mechanisms for exposing investors and founders to each other—frequently forums or clubs that provide entrepreneurs with a presentation window at a monthly or quarterly meeting to multiple angel investors along with other would-be CEOs. It's a lot like speed dating, and if you choose this route, make sure that you have a solid presentation that you've tested with as many people as you can. As the saying goes, you only get one chance to make a first impression. You need to be able to present your vision and business plan in a nontechnical way that conveys to the audience what your product is, who the customers are, what the competition is, and why your product will be successful in the market-place. Unless you're presenting to an audience of fellow nerds, always remember that nobody gives a crap what microprocessor or operating system you are using unless it is absolutely critical to your success and competitive advantage.

This may be a good time to present some guidelines for success-ful presentations using PowerPoint, as it is pretty much the default program for making presentations to large groups. Over the years I've given hundreds of presentations to all kinds of groups, from a handful of customers to hundreds of engineers, and I've developed a few tech-niques that make presentations more effective and easier to prepare. When building a PowerPoint, there are some things to keep in mind.

- **Purpose.** Make sure that you understand the people you are presenting to and why they are there. The only thing worse than standing in front of three hundred people for a presentation is realizing a couple of minutes in that what you prepared is of no interest whatsoever—could be the longest thirty minutes of your life.

- **PowerPoint is a tool.** You are doing the presentation, and the PowerPoint is primarily a tool to keep you on track and convey the most important points. Anyone who has ever sat through a half hour of someone reading what is on the screen knows just how painful it can be. Bullet points and graphics are wonderful tools to communicate critical points, but essay-length sentences kill effectiveness.

- **Fonts.** Use different fonts and colors to provide clarity, reduce monotony, and make sure that the font is large enough to be seen from fifty to seventy-five yards away (note: this will also force you to be brief to fit it all on a page).

- **Repetition.** You know that every word you say is profound, but keep in mind that your audience won't remember even a fraction of what you say, so make sure that key points and themes are presented multiple times in different variations. If the key competitive advantage to your product is that it is faster and will save your customers time and money, make sure that you say that in different ways several times in your presentation. Tell 'em what you're going to tell 'em, tell 'em, and then tell 'em what you told 'em.

- **Brevity.** Once you are told that you will have fifteen or thirty minutes or whatever to address a few hundred folks, you will likely find yourself waking up in cold sweats from a recurring nightmare: eight minutes into the presentation, and you are on your last slide. The logical cure is to put together a volume of slides that will ensure that you do not end up with ten minutes of awkward silence in the room. Unfortunately, this will also ensure that your message is completely lost, and you will present your last ten slides in roughly forty-five seconds and become a laughingstock among your peers. To prevent this, I have a simple technique: once you have all the slides you think you need, delete half of them. Then take what's left and delete half of those. Now do a run-through of your presentation and add any slides that are absolutely necessary to get your point across—and add these very grudgingly. Trust me, it works—and by the way, you can use a similar technique when packing for a trip: put the clothes you want to take on the bed and put half of them back, then put half of what's left back, and then add in anything you absolutely, positively have to take.

- **Relax.** Easier said than done, and I can honestly say that after almost forty years of giving presentations, I still get nervous before I speak (but it does get better). There are only two ways to get better at public speaking: give bad presentations and give good presentations. The key thing to remind yourself is that you were invited to speak for a reason and have some information that someone thought was useful to the audience. They aren't there to judge you as an entertainer; they are there to hear the information that you have that will be beneficial to them, so their focus is on the message, not the messenger. I've heard people talk about gimmicks like picturing your audience in their underwear, but in my experience that is either disgusting or distracting (if you know what I mean), so I wouldn't bother. What does help for me is to keep moving my eyes around the audience and making eye contact with as many people as possible. This is a good practice for any presenter as it creates a connection with the audience, but it also serves to help you stay calm. While you are making eye contact around the room, you will (hopefully) come across some folks who respond with a smile or nod their heads in agreement with something you said. Remember where these folks are in the crowd, and if you hit a rough spot, look back to them for reassurance that you are getting the message across.

It goes without saying that this is by no means an exhaustive list of alternatives for raising capital (for example, lotteries, sperm donation, breaking bad), but as with everything else in this book, you need to put on your creative hat and come up with a source or sources that meet your needs and situation.

So how did our friend Dave Lavin solve the funding problem? As you may recall, when we last left Dave, he had figured out how big the market was, what share he thought (hoped) he could get in five years, and how much money he would need to get through the first year or so. Obviously there are a lot more details that need to go into a business plan (sales, engineering, production, finance, etc.), but as our focus here is on money and the acquisition thereof, we will leave the details of Dave's plan till later, when we consider each of the areas separately. With the help of his golfing buddy and accountant Mark (and a bill for $800 he had to explain to Maggie), he put together a reasonably sound plan that he could take to Maggie and get buy-in. Being a fast learner, he opted to skip the smart-ass remarks and subtlety and instead took her out for a nice dinner at her favorite restaurant, where laid out the plan for her. Let's pick up our story after Dave has gone through the plan with her and is waiting for her reaction.

After heaving a deep sigh, Maggie looks Dave in the eyes and says, "OK, first let me say that I'm really impressed with the work you've done on the plan, but it would have been nice if you'd mentioned the eight-hundred-dollar bill from your friend Mark."

"Yeah, I know, but I was kind of hoping he might be willing to hold off on that till we could do the AC work, but the parts didn't come in."

"Whatever. The important part is that if, *and I do mean if,* we decide to go ahead with this, you better make damn sure that I don't have eight-hundred-dollar surprises showing up in the mail-box. Period!"

"I know, and I'm sorry—it won't happen again, but what do you think about the plan?"

"Like I said, I think the plan is pretty good, but I have a few questions, starting with where the hell are you planning to get a quarter of a million dollars? Unless you hit the mega jackpot and I missed it, we don't have it. In fact, we don't have a fraction of that, so what's the plan?" she asks.

"Needless to say, I've been thinking about that a lot, and I've got some ideas. I figure between checking and savings, we've got about eight thousand dollars."

"And unless I'm missing something, you need about twenty thousand a month, so we have enough for about ten days."

"Wait, I'm not done yet. I've still got my Christmas bonus, which is probably going to be about ten thousand dollars," Dave tells her.

"OK, so we can survive for almost a whole month, and from what I can see the company isn't going to be throwing off a lot of income in the first month, so—"

"I know, I know. But we also have the 401(k) from Hackman, and that's almost thirty-eight thousand dollars, so we really have almost fifty grand to work with."

"OK…so what you're saying is, we risk everything we've spent ten years saving, and it will pay for less than three months of expenses, and we're still at least ten months from even having a product to sell? Am I missing something?"

Dave knows he's hit the weak point in his presentation, so he opts for some flattery. "As usual, Mag, you figured that out pretty quickly."

"Sucking up doesn't change the math, so can it and get back to the manure you're getting ready to spread."

"Got it, my bad. I had a few ideas about where to get the money that I've been fooling around with—"

"Had? Meaning past tense? Had, meaning no longer viable?" she asks.

"Sort of, but give me a chance. I figured I would start by seeing if we could find a few friends and relatives who would put up ten thousand dollars each for a small percentage of ownership, and we could use that money to get us through. I sort of started some exploratory discussions with some folks as kind of a trial balloon."

"Might have been nice to let me know that was going on, but are you saying that you've found twenty people who are interested?"

"Not exactly," he says uncomfortably.

"Apparently you've forgotten our last 'not exactly' discussion," she tells him, eyebrows raised.

"Oh. Yeah. Sorry. But anyway, it hasn't worked out quite as well as I had hoped."

"Remarkably vague. How many investors have you lined up? Exactly how many?"

"Um, I've got two maybes so far," he replies.

"Two maybes. Excuse me if I seem somewhat underwhelmed."

"Yeah, me too. I think by the time I line up enough folks, the chance to get into this market will have passed us by."

"Well, I have to say that I'm glad you gave it a try, but I'm sort of relieved that we're not going to step off a cliff right now," she begins.

"Whoa, whoa, not so fast—I've got another idea," he protests.

"I'm listening," she replies.

"You know, old man Hackman has more money than God, and he's always looking for new investments."

"You can't be serious. You're really thinking of walking into Ed's office, telling him you're quitting, and then asking if he'd mind giving you the money for the new company that you're leaving for? No offense, but that's gonna take some big cojones, and I know your anatomy well enough to know you ain't got 'em."

"Well, yeah, when you say it like that it does sound like a bit of a stretch. But Ed knows that I'm not happy; and if I'm leaving anyway, this gives him a chance to make some money off my departure, and we can still work together…sort of."

"And have you talked to him yet?" she asks.

"Of course not! I would never take such an important step without consulting you first."

"Right. Let's just say your track record on that isn't exactly stellar so far, but back to the topic at hand. I think the plan is pretty good, and I can see that you're very excited about this. I'm not sure I buy into your thinking about Ed, but you obviously know him better than I do, so I guess I'm in. My only request is that you take some time and think about this before you go and talk to Ed since it's really blah… blah…blah…"

Of course, everything after "I'm in" was just noise. And of course Dave waited about nine hours before he asked Ed to have a beer with him after work. Our story picks up at the Goosed Moose Bar & Grille later that day.

"Hey, Ed, thanks for taking the time to meet with me on such short notice," says Dave.

"No problem, but why so formal? And how come we couldn't just meet at the office during the day?" Ed asks.

"Well, I wanted to talk to you about something that I really didn't want anybody else to hear, and I figured this way we could talk freely."

"OK, Dave, I think I see where this is going, so let me see if I can guess: I know you have had some problems with Rick since he got back from school, and I understand where you're coming from. I know he's got a lot to learn, and I appreciate that you've been patient in trying to work with him. I think he's making progress, and I hope you're not thinking of doing anything drastic."

"Well, you're certainly right that I've had some issues with Rick, and I certainly have been concerned about my future and place at Hackman now that he's back, and I guess maybe that's part of why I wanted to meet—but actually I have something else to run by you. And I'd like you to hear me out before you react."

"Hell, we've known each other for what, ten years now? I think it's safe to say at this point there isn't much we can't throw out on the table and talk about—fire away."

"Fair enough. Now you know that since I got my degree, I've been working on some projects on nights and weekends. I think I mentioned that I had some ideas for a new thermostat/controller for residential jobs that could save a bunch of energy."

"You haven't exactly shared a lot of details, but yeah, you told me you had something you were working on."

"I've actually spent a lot of time on it and have a prototype ready. It's got a lot of algorithms I wrote that look like they will save at least 20 percent of the energy used by a typical house and also have learning features that could save even more."

"You've got my attention. I'm assuming that you want the OK to put these in some of our customers' homes, right?"

"Well, that's certainly part of what I'm thinking about, but there's more."

"Jesus Christ, boy, am I going to have to reach down your throat and drag out the rest of it? I'm not getting any younger, you know, so just spill it, OK?"

"OK, here's the deal. I've been looking into this, and I think this has real potential in the market, and I want to take a shot at running my own company," Dave says.

"So you're quitting?" Ed exclaims.

"No! Well, yes. Maybe. Look, just let me finish, all right? Like I said, I want to start a company, and I've got a business plan put together. The thing is, I have everything ready to go, and I've got some cash put aside, but it's not enough, and—"

"And you're thinking that I might be willing to put up a few bucks to get this off the ground."

"Pretty much, yeah."

"How much?"

"Well, I need a total of about two hundred fifty thousand, and I figure I've got about fifty, so I'm looking for someone to invest about two hundred thousand."

"OK, so what does two hundred large get me?" Ed asks.

"I was thinking about ten percent."

"I'm thinking we should get the check and forget this ever happened. The deal you're offering me is that I put up two hundred thousand and own ten percent, and you put up fifty thousand and get ninety percent. I like you, Dave, but this is not happening for anything close to what you're thinking."

"So what are you thinking?"

"I think you had the percentages right, just in the wrong order, but let's look at this from a math standpoint: I figure if I put up eighty percent of the money, I get eighty percent of the equity. That seems fair to me—but keep in mind, I haven't agreed to anything yet. If we can come up with numbers that work, I'd be willing to look at the plan you've put together."

"Look, Ed, I've got a ton of hours into this already, and that's got to be worth a lot, since none of this happens without the work I've done. So I'm thinking sixty for me and forty for you. How's that sound?" Dave asks.

"Sounds like you have some other money lined up that you should go after."

"I've got other people who are interested, but I wanted to give you first shot at this, since you've always been good to me."

"I'm deeply touched…seventy-thirty."

"OK, I'm glad you're interested, and I'd really like to see this happen, so why don't we just split it fifty-fifty. Fair for both of us, right?"

"Fair, but stupid. If everybody's in charge, nobody's in charge. I'll put my cards on the table—this sounds like fun, and I'd like to at least see what you've got, so here's my final offer: sixty-forty to me. If I look at the plan, and there's something more, I'd be willing to sweeten the pot a little, but that's it."

"I'm really ready to get going, so OK for now. I think once you see what I've got, we may have to revisit the numbers."

"Fair enough. Give me the plan, and Rick and I will take a look at it and see if we're interested," Ed tells him.

Oh shit!

"So you're thinking Rick would invest too?"

"I'm actually thinking that Rick might be a lot more involved in this than I will be."

Oh shit! Oh shit!

"What do you mean, 'more involved'?"

"Well, Rick and I have been talking, since he got his degree at CU in marketing, about how he really doesn't have much of a chance to use what he's learned at the shop."

Oh shit! Oh shit! Oh shit!

"So what are you thinking?"

"I'm thinking this is a win-win. Rick gets to cut his teeth at something new, and you get a bunch of money and a partner to handle the sales and marketing for free. You get to save a ton of money and focus on what you do best—technical stuff. Perfect!"

Oh shit! Oh shit! Oh shit! Oh shit!

"Look, Ed, I like Rick well enough, and he's a smart kid and all, but he doesn't have any experience at anything like this, and I'm really not sure—" Dave begins.

"Don't bother blowing sunshine up my ass, OK? I'll deny I ever said this, but you and I both know the kid is not doing me any favors at the shop, and if you leave there's nobody there to keep him from becoming a total train wreck but me. I've already got my hands full, so this is a package deal. You get the money and Rick, I get him out of my hair for you to deal with, and he gets to be in charge of his own deal," Ed says in a satisfied tone.

Oh shit! Oh shit! Oh shit! Oh shit! Oh shit!

"Rick's going to be in charge?" Dave asks.

"Of course not. Between you and me, you'll be the one calling the shots, and I'll back whatever you want to do. He'll just have some title, but he'll really only be in charge of sales and marketing and anything else you want him to do."

"I gotta tell you, Ed—I think I'm up to about five or six 'oh shits' in my head right now. But I think you've probably figured out that I don't have a ton of options, so why don't you take the business plan and look at it, and we can get back together in a couple of days and discuss it."

"Probably have to be next week. Rick's going to be out of town till Monday."

"Didn't he take Monday off this week?"

"Don't start. Give me the plan, and I'll get back to you if I have any questions."

"Since you've pretty much pantsed me in front of the whole bar, will you at least pick up the tab?" Dave asks.

"Sure, partner," says Ed with a chuckle.

Oh shit! Oh shit! Oh shit! Oh shit! Oh shit! Oh shit!

Remember the Golden Rule: "He who has the gold makes the rules."

I won't keep you in suspense, Dave took the deal, but he did manage to get a couple of concessions—they would draw off Ed's money first, and after the first six months, if things were going well, Dave could draw a salary of three grand a month. A small victory, but at least it was something.

6

BE CAREFUL WHAT YOU WISH FOR

Congratulations! You've learned new ways to grovel, put your pride in cold storage, and sold your soul to the devil. But you got your funding, and now you can start to do something productive.

The good news is that you get to run your own company. The bad news is that you have to run your own company.

If you slept like a baby last night and don't feel completely overwhelmed by the task in front of you, you're either a much better person than I am or you have no idea what you have gotten yourself into. There are so many things on your plate that it is hard to know where to start, but the best thing to do is to break the big jobs down into manageable tasks, much like we did with the financial analysis we put together a while back. To this point, your sole focus (quite correctly) has been on getting funding in place as nothing else matters if you don't have the dough. Get ready to take the first refreshing sip from the fire hose you'll be drinking from for the next year or so.

You might be fired up about buying some new equipment or computers or laptops or whatever, but to start your company on the right track, you need to shift your focus from internal needs to external issues. Now is the time to realize that you need to start making your company look much larger and credible than it really is (try to view your company as someone would from the outside and see what that person's perspective is). If this doesn't sound important, let me paint a picture for you. Imagine that you're a few months into the business and you are ready to close your first deal. The customer is getting ready to send back your signed quote and sees that the reply to address in the email is horndog151@hotmail.com (and if you think this hasn't happened, trust me, it has). If you were the customer, do you think that you might have second thoughts committing thousands of dollars to this company? This might seem trivial now, but it damn sure better be on your list. So what does that list look like? Obviously, it's going to depend a lot on the details of your business, but let's consider a few generic items that should be on almost anybody's list:

- Office space
- Furniture
- Business cards
- Network/IT
- Network support
- Phones
- Business name and registration with the state
- Domain name(s)
- Website
- Trademarks
- Copyrights
- Patents
- Attorney
- Accountant
- Accounting software
- Contact management software
- Development software
- Productivity software (Office, OpenOffice, etc.)
- Bank account
- Production tools
- Test equipment
- Packaging materials
- Coffee maker
- Microwave

I realize that some of the things on this list may seem trivial, but believe me when I say that one or more of them will bite you in the ass at some point, and you will find yourself scrambling to put things together on short notice. The thing to keep in mind is that some things are absolutely essential and nonnegotiable (for example, product quality), but even things that don't directly affect your product or customers need to send a consistent message of quality, reliability and staying power to your customers, employees, vendors, and partners. You may think now that product performance and features are the most critical to your long-term success, but you may be surprised to learn that one of the biggest challenges to getting customers is their concern that you may not be around for the long haul. Both of my companies made products that were integrated into my customers' systems, which meant that if my products failed or I went out of business, my customers could be left with unhappy customers; so they want to know not only that your products have great features but also that they have high reliability and that you will be around to stand behind your products down the road. So how do you manage to send the right message without blowing the budget? Let's take a look at a few of the items on our list and see how it works.

Office Space

Waste money on office space—what for? Why not save the dough and stay in your basement for a few months? There are a lot of reasons, but the main one is that you need a clear delineation between your home life and work. Until now it's been OK to have the kids coming in to ask for help with their homework or running upstairs to make a sandwich, but you are now the owner of a company, and you need to not only have a place to work but also keep regular hours and not wear your bathrobe when you sit down to start pounding code. Psychologically, having an office sets you and your employees in the right frame of mind: "I'm going to work, see you tonight."

This is probably a good time to let you in on a little secret: the biggest single impediment to the growth of your company is not cash, competitors, or market conditions. If you'd like to know what is going to keep you from having a company with $10 million in revenue in a few years, just step into the bathroom and take a nice long look in the mirror. If you can't visualize the huge growth potential of your company, then it simply won't happen. I can't tell you how many entrepreneurs I have worked with who have unintentionally created obstacles to growth in a variety of ways. Just one quick example: I worked with one company that manufactured current transformers that we needed for out electrical submeter line. We wanted to purchase a transformer that they made with a very slight modification (a different resistor value, for anyone who cares) that would add no additional time or cost to the build. The only cost to the company was the time required to modify the build documentation, and we had already paid a one-time cost of $1,000 to get that completed. The work was all done, and the only thing standing between them and our first order for several thousand dollars was sign-off by the CEO. No one else could sign off, despite the fact that this company not only had a VP of sales but also a VP of engineering. The founder and CEO was on a sailboat somewhere in the South Pacific and totally unreachable (keep in mind, this was twenty-plus years ago when it actually was possible to be unreachable). No one knew exactly when he would check in, and even if he called and gave a verbal OK, no one could proceed with the order before receiving a hard copy with his signature. Now, this was likely a legacy of the company's earlier days when the founder was the engineering and sales department, but he had failed to see that (a) his company had grown substantially, and other people should have the authority to approve minor changes; and (b) he had enough income to spend three months in the South Seas. We ended up buying from another vendor on a short-term basis that turned into over $2 million in the next five years—oops.

We'll talk some more about office space for a couple of reasons: first, it is something that most people aren't familiar with, and a lot of the terms may be confusing; and second, many of the principles we use in making a real estate deal will apply more broadly to other areas we will explore. If you still don't know why you need to spend time and money on office space, take the time you would have spent on this and use it to update your résumé as you will probably need it sooner rather than later. Here are a few key points about office space leasing that you should know:

- **Personal guarantees.** Let's just get this one on the table now as it will save you a great deal of heartache and frustration later on. To get any lease on office space, you will need to provide a personal guarantee to the landlord. This is essentially a promise that you will be personally responsible for paying the rent regardless of whether your company goes belly-up or not. If you're like I was the first time I ran in to this, your immediate reaction is to call bullshit—after all, you're not renting the space, your company is; and besides, you just spent all that time and effort raising capital, so the money is not going to be any problem. Before you freak out, put yourself in the landlord's shoes. The LLC you set up is designed to protect you from personal liability for the company, and any landlord knows this—and knows that you can just shut things down any time and walk away, leaving him or her with space that is technically leased but not generating any income. If this logic doesn't help you, get over it, because you have no option other than prepaying all the rent; and we all know that's not happening. And believe me, this is not the last time you will have to do it. I bring this up now because you will have options to get cheaper rent for a longer term, but realize that you could end up writing personal checks for space you don't use long after your company goes belly-up, so be very careful.
- **Use a broker.** A commercial real estate broker knows the market and knows where to find the kind of space you need and also can help you navigate some of the unfamiliar terms you will encounter. Besides, the landlord pays the broker fees, so

it doesn't cost you anything to use one; and a broker will save you all kinds of time that you don't have right now, so just take my word for it.

- **Type of space to look for.** You may recall from an earlier chapter that I commented somewhat derisively on the VC-funded start-up that hadn't made a dime but occupied high-end Class A office space in the heart of downtown. Does that mean that I don't think a start-up should ever look at expensive high-end space? Pretty much, yeah. The only exception would be if you needed to get a specific space for competitive reasons—for example, if you are running one of those wunderkind dot-com social media companies, you may feel it's necessary to get some of that uber-cool loft space with room for the beanbag chairs and espresso machines in order to recruit coding talent. OK, but if you're doing it because of your ego or because you want space that will make your mom proud when she brings her book club around, don't do it. For the most part, "mixed use" or industrial space in the suburbs will rent for a third or less of what downtown space goes for, and cash flow is everything at this point.

- **How much space do you need?** When you do start looking for space, remember that you have a business plan that calls for very high growth in the first few years, and the last thing you want to do is have to try to get out of your lease and move in the middle of the second year. Of course, you also do not want to take on a whole lot more space than you need. It's very useful to look around when you are shopping for space and see if there is adjacent vacant space that the landlord might give you first right of refusal on as part of the lease. You can easily expand with a minimum of disruption without committing cash you don't want to spend. Another alternative is to talk to the landlord about additional space that he or she may have in the same complex (or another) that you could move to without any penalties on the existing lease. Depending on market conditions, this may be a win-win for both you and the landlord.

- **Triple net (NNN) lease terms.** Most leases are what are referred to as triple net leases. This basically means that in addition to the rent, you will be responsible for taxes, maintenance, and utilities. The nonutility part of this will come in the form of CAM (common area maintenance) costs, which will be charged monthly and are usually adjusted on an annual basis. These costs per square foot will be disclosed to you in the lease agreement for prior years, so you can factor this into the total cost of your space.
- **Tenant improvement (TI) work.** Let's say you find a space that fits your needs, but the layout isn't quite right—too much office space, not enough production square footage, and so on. Most landlords will work with you to design a space that fits what you want and roll the TI costs into your rent, which will save you large capital outlays and spread the cost of the TI work over a longer term. On the other hand, if you are willing to work with what the landlord has with minimal changes, you can negotiate a lower lease rate in exchange for accepting less-than-ideal layouts.
- **Lease term.** The longer the term you are willing to sign up for, the lower the rate the landlord will accept (don't forget your personal guarantee). One of the things you can usually do is negotiate a lease with built-in escalators that allow you to pay a lower rate in the early years and more in the later years. This can be very attractive as you are able to match the increase in rents with growth in the company and pay the higher rents when you are making more money down the road. In some cases, you can even "backload" your lease with significantly higher rents in later years under certain circumstances—for example, when I negotiated the lease for new space (knowing that I intended to sell the company before the lease was up), I backloaded the lease so that my costs up front were much lower than they would be later, which helped to improve the net income when we went to sell (remember earnings multiples on sale?). Of course, the rent for future years had to be disclosed

in due diligence to the buyers so they were fully informed, but it worked to my advantage when it came time to negotiate the sales price. You may also have leverage with the landlord under some circumstances—on one of my leases, I was working with a landlord, and the broker knew that he wanted to put the building on the market and having more space leased made the building more attractive to a buyer; so I was able to get a rate that was probably 75 percent of that of comparable properties in the area. Just keep in mind that everything is negotiable, so make the lease fit your needs.

- **Cable and infrastructure for IT and comms.** Putting in wires for phones and networks can be ridiculously expensive and is usually a cost borne by the renter. When you are looking at potential space, make sure to look and see if the previous tenant left behind infrastructure that may be useful: phone and computer cabling and jacks, switches, UPS power supplies, and so on. One word of caution: you'd be amazed at the amount of time and labor tenants will put in to removing cables and other equipment when they leave so don't assume that just because there are wall plates with phone and network jacks that the stuff behind the walls is useful or even present; and if this is important to you, spend the time and/or money to look behind the walls and verify what's there.

Network, Software, and Comms

If you are a computer geek or have one on your staff, the odds are that you have most of the equipment you need to get your network running. It may not be pretty, but if you can figure out a way to get things going with what you have (especially when you do not have a ton of employees on the system), you can save yourself a ton of time and money that is better spent on product-related activities.

Most engineers and software folks have PCs at home that would be the envy of many Fortune 500 companies and also have copies of software that you will need for development (all fully licensed, of course, as I would never endorse using any form of bootleg software just because it's free). As I have no desire to have a forced colonoscopy from Microsoft's lawyers (I hear they don't even use lubricants), I will repeat that I absolutely do not endorse using any unlicensed software just because it's free, OK? Another note on software: you may be tempted at this point to get by with open-source software, and it can be fine for some things (I happen to think OpenOffice does 90 percent of what you need for word processing), but give some thought to things like accounting and customer resource management (CRM) software on the front end. Cutting corners now may prove very costly later on as you try to port customer records from one system to another or lose valuable data because your software isn't adequate.

You may be tempted to go to Costco and pick up a five-phone wireless system, but before you do that, look on eBay and Amazon for used phone switches—they can handle multiple lines and provide additional features that may prove very useful much sooner than you think. Most are also expandable, so you can add more lines and handsets and features like voicemail as your needs grow. If you buy used equipment from a reputable dealer, it will provide a warranty and support if needed, and this gear is much cheaper than buying new. Yes, it may be obsolete in a couple of years, but if you buy a name brand, the odds are you can upgrade to newer gear with minimal hassle and defer the cost for a few years. If you can squeeze four years out of some used gear, you are well ahead of the game.

Office Furniture

One word: USED. You would be surprised at the value you can get buying used office cubes, desks, and so on in very good condition. This is one of those areas where you can really stretch your dollars and still make a very good impression on customers or other visitors who may visit your office. Keep in mind that new office furnishings are used office furnishings the day after they are installed; used stuff can cost one-third or less of new, and most sellers will let you pick through their inventory to get the best stuff there is. You may also get lucky by hitting one of the surplus locations of large companies in your area (Intel, Microsoft, etc.) as most of them have locations for surplus office furnishings and even computer gear.

Intellectual Property

Hopefully you've already done most of this, but if not, now is the time to make sure you get everything registered and protected. I am often amazed at how far people have gotten down the road with a start-up without covering their asses. You are going to be producing valuable products and other intellectual property that others will try to copy or steal in the not-too-distant future, so make sure you have yourself covered on at least these things:

- **Company name.** Before you file the paperwork with the state to register your company, make sure that you have at least done a cursory search to see if the name you have chosen is already claimed by someone else. Using a name that infringes on some other company can not only be expensive but can also cause a great deal of embarrassment for you and confusion for your customers a few years along. A long discussion about the type of company you form is beyond the scope of this book, but the most likely candidates are LLCs (limited liability corporations) and subchapter S corporations, both of which are relatively easy to set up and have minimal ongoing obligations for reporting and taxes. This is a great time to find a lawyer you are comfortable with as he or she can provide some advice on company structure and take care of most of the paperwork and hassles. There are several schools of thought on what kind of name to pick for your company. You can pick something descriptive of what you do, or something cute and clever, or some obscure Latin term modified to be catchy but not infringing. This is what I did—in the case of my last company, the name is a Latin term for a gate or opening in a wall, and because the company was building a gateway to energy information, it always made for a great story and is memorable. Pretty clever, huh?

- **Trademarks and copyrights.** I have to confess that I've never been entirely clear on where trademarks stop and copyrights begin (or vice versa), but my thinking has always been that you trademark product names and copyright written materials and software—please consult your attorney. I'm of the opinion that you have very similar options for naming products as you do for naming your company. I've always favored something that alludes to how the product is used but is also clever and unique enough to be memorable. My first company made products for measuring energy consumption, and the products had names like Enercept, Enspector, and so on. My last company makes products for data acquisition (AcquiSuite) and frequency-hopping Modbus communications (ModHopper)—sounds corny, but you would be amazed at how catchy names help customers remember your products much better than if you call them something like R4560-T100. As a side note, all of the products had a product number (like R4569-T100) that provided descriptive information about the product's rating or features, but all of them fell under the umbrella of the product family name. Regardless of what naming scheme you use, now is the time to get not only those names but any others that are similar trademarked, because you may want to use them later; and you also want to prevent competitors from introducing a competing product with a very similar name. It's not very expensive and will provide you much peace of mind down the road.

- **Patents.** Few things in this world are more time-consuming, frustrating, and expensive than writing and filing patents on products, but this will also prove to be the best time and money you spend if your company and products are successful. Patents not only serve to keep competitors from copying your products but also can add significant value to your company when it comes time to sell. It may seem trivial, but large companies place a huge value on IP, particularly IP that is protected by one or more patents; so bite the bullet and do it. There are a few things that you can do to make this process less painful (most of which I have learned the hard way at no small cost). First, do a cursory search on the US Patent and Trademark Office (USPTO) on your own before you engage an IP attorney, as he or she will charge you $150 an hour to have some paralegal do the same search you can do for free. It's not an exhaustive search, and you will have to pay somebody to do it later, but you may discover that the incredibly brilliant and new idea you have has already been done and claimed by someone else, and you may have to shift gears a bit to work around what somebody else has already patented. Assuming it looks like you're OK, it's time to hire an IP lawyer—sadly, probably a different lawyer than the one who filed your corporate paperwork with the state, as you need someone who specializes in this stuff. On my first few patents, I made the mistake of handing the lawyer a fairly brief description of the product and applications and any unique features that I thought had value. What I discovered was that because the lawyers had limited experience with our products and technologies, my engineers and I spent far more time rewriting what the attorney had prepared than we would have if we simply wrote it ourselves in the first place (and still spent $150 or more per hour). For my later products, I would simply download a copy of a successful patent for a similar product and cut and paste in the details of my product, reusing the legal BS and filler that they need. I would then give this to the attorney to do some fine-tuning and add the information about the patent search they do and any references to "prior art" (stuff somebody else already did that was similar and why our product was different). A full discussion of patenting is well beyond our scope, but just know that you will have multiple rewrites and frustration, as some clerk in the patent office makes you jump through more hoops than a trained seal.

- **Domain names and websites.** Please tell me that you've already looked into websites (keeping in mind that the ideal domain name is the same as the company name you protected earlier). The further away you have to get from something like jimscompany.com, the more difficult it will be for customers to find you later on. If you can't do an exact match, avoid the temptation to do something long and clever—nobody wants to type in a whole ton of letters and numbers to find you. Just because someone has the domain name you want, don't lose hope— many companies buy a bunch of names to protect them, or they may start using a name and the company fails, so the site isn't active. Do a Google search and see if the site is really active, and if it's not find out who owns it and contact them. You may be able to buy the name and even though it seems expensive it is well worth it if you can get exactly the URL you want. The good news about website design is that there are a lot of relatively inexpensive resources out there to get your website up and running. Just remember that this is the face of your company for customers, partners, and vendors, so it needs to be useful as well as professional to present the image you want. You can choose to host the site yourself or farm it out to a data center; and unless you have a particular reason to keep it in-house, I would move hosting to somebody else.
- **Logo.** Sooner or later you are going to need a company logo for your website, business cards, letterhead, invoices, and so on, so you might as well do it now. This is an area where I'm OK with doing it yourself if you are reasonable creative (or have a friend or family member who is). I designed the logo for my last company, and it lasted with minor iterations for ten years till I sold the company. Keep in mind that unlike the company name or patents, you can change your logo pretty easily without much need for approvals by government regulators, so don't kill yourself on this one.

Attorney(s) and Accountant(s)

I've already mentioned the need for these folks—and yes, I hate them as much as you do, but they are absolutely essential. A good lawyer and accountant will bring you enormous peace of mind and will probably save you a fortune down the road. Your best source is a referral from someone you know who is in a similar situation and has someone he or she would refer without hesitation. I know you have a friend or lodge buddy who did your will a few years ago and says he can handle the corporate stuff with no problem, but this is not the time to let friendship cloud your judgment. First of all, any lawyer worth his salt will be the first to tell you that you don't use a family lawyer to do corporate work any more than you would go to a family doctor for heart surgery—they're both doctors, but one does the surgery several times a week, and the other is probably going to have to put a book with step-by-step instructions on your chest while she works. Thank him for the offer and go get the guy who can do this in his sleep. Same with accountants—the one down the street who does your taxes may not be the best choice for corporate work. You need somebody who not only can do your taxes but also can set up your accounting software and help you make decisions as you go along to minimize the taxes and paperwork based on your corporate structure.

So how did our buddy Dave handle these issues? For once he was very lucky—turns out that when Ed bought the building for the refrigeration company, he also bought a small adjacent building that he had been using primarily for storage of his RV and some old cars he collected. He told Dave that he would be willing to let the company use the space rent-free as long as they covered the CAM charges, which were minimal. The space needed some cleaning up, and it certainly wasn't a place to impress customers (or moms), but saving three or four grand a month made it worthwhile for now; and there was no long-term lease, so when things took off, he could easily move to nicer digs on short notice.

Dave had a computer with all the software he needed for development (fully licensed, of course), and as the building didn't really have finished walls, he could easily handle the wiring necessary to get up and running and build a functioning network. The only real drawback was that the best he could do for comms was a DSL line, but the phone company was willing to make a bundled deal that was very cost-effective. He went out and bought a copy of QuickBooks (licensed, of course) and a contact management software called Gold Mine (licensed, of course) so Rick could have access to a customer database for his sales efforts. As Dave was bringing his computer and software to the company, he naturally assumed that Rick would bring his existing laptop from Hackman, and they could get up and running quickly with little expense. Dave is about to learn a valuable lesson about partners (especially those born with silver spoons). Dave starts the conversation by sharing his thoughts. "Since I have a computer at home that has plenty of horsepower and already has the code for the product, I figured I would bring that in and save some cash. I assume there's no problem with you bringing the laptop from Hackman, right?"

Rick says, "I'm sure Dad wouldn't care, but that's a secondhand computer that I got from the office manager when I came back from school, and I really don't think it will be good enough. I've tried to tell the old man that for months, but you know what a cheap bastard he can be at times."

"OK, I guess I don't see what's wrong with it other than it's not brand new."

"For starters, it takes forever to boot up, and I really hate the keyboard. You're the one who keeps harping on quality and appearance, so how would it look it I went to see a big customer and I couldn't do my presentation because my POS computer crashed? Boom! Huge sale down the drain, and I don't want to risk that."

"OK, OK. We've got bigger fish to fry, so let's get this out of the way. I saw a really nice desktop PC at Costco this weekend for eight hundred dollars. Plenty of horsepower and comes with Windows and even a starter copy of Office, so I'll just—"

"Whoa there, cowboy! I'm not starting this venture with some off-the-shelf, off-brand piece of crap—we need to have some standards here."

"Well, it is off the shelf, but I'm not sure that HP would appreciate being referred to as off-brand, and it will do what we want at the right price."

"Might do what you want, but I've got something else in mind. I was over visiting a buddy of mine a couple of days ago, and he's got the setup we need. It's a Lenovo ThinkPad with a full docking station and a couple of nineteen-inch monitors. Very cool, he can have an email open on one screen and be looking at the customer screen in the CRM at the same time. He's got a dedicated Epson 3880 printer for high quality marketing materials, which is exactly what we need," says Rick.

"Wow, sounds cool, but also sounds pretty expensive, so maybe we should—" Dave begins.

"Way ahead of you, Dave. Found everything on Amazon Prime with free shipping, and it will be here tomorrow morning."

"How much are we talking about?"

"Don't remember exactly, but the laptop was about three."

"Thousand?"

"Duh, of course thousand. Anyway, the docking station was around a grand, and the monitors were something like a thousand each, and the printer was maybe fifteen hundred with additional ink cartridges, so all in we're only looking at maybe seventy-five hundred. Oh, and I got a case to protect it when I travel, so call it eight grand even."

"And you didn't think you needed to run this by me?"

"Why? It's a marketing expense, so why do I need your OK?"

"Well, for starters, we're partners in this, and I need to have input before we spend this kind of money on toys."

"Just because this equipment isn't for engineering doesn't mean that they are toys. And let's be clear—I own sixty percent of this company, and I don't intend to clear every expense with you—end of story."

Suffice to say that two things happened today: Dave learned a valuable lesson about being a minority shareholder, and Maggie learned that night that the word motherf***er could be used as a noun, verb, adjective, adverb, and gerund in a single sentence.

7

PEOPLE YOU WORK WITH

I realize that the title of this chapter is a bit clumsy at best, but I have my reasons for using it. Terms like *employees, coworkers,* and, of course, the ever-trendy *team members* are reasonably useful in many contexts, but you are working with a much wider variety of people than just those who work for you and are (at least theoretically) expected to carry out your every wish. In your new role of entrepreneur, you will need to work with not only employees, customers, investors, and vendors, you are likely to also have to deal with one class of coworker that is very unfamiliar: fellow owners. There are two classes of fellow owners: minority shareholders and majority shareholders. For your sake, I hope that you were able to hold onto a majority position because, in many cases, minority shareholders are treated with somewhat less respect and consideration than your average migrant farm worker—much more on this later, but just be aware that having fellow equity owners creates a burden unique to the start-up world.

First let's talk a little bit about employees. I know there are all kinds of PC things you are supposed to call them to make them feel more included, up to and including one company that refers to employees as family members. I don't know about your family, but I have family members I hate to call family members, and I refuse to bestow the title on people I not only just met but also pay to be around me. This is in no way intended to downplay the importance of people you hire—simply put, they will either make or break your new venture, and each hire is absolutely critical. You need to make clear right from the start that you will only hire the very best people around and that you won't tolerate mediocrity. You will make mistakes, of course, but this is one of those cases where mistakes can be turned to your advantage—when (not if) you do hire a dud, correct the mistake swiftly and decisively. This is not the time to get soft and mushy and kind-hearted and be the benevolent leader.

If this sounds harsh, there are several reasons why you have to move quickly when it turns out you made a hiring boo-boo:

1. **Money:** cash flow is everything in a small company, and I virtually guarantee that you will find yourself scrambling to meet payroll many times in the early years. The only thing worse than paying for top talent and performance is pissing away money on people who aren't performing, Might as well take it out to the parking lot and burn it—at least you'd get warm.

2. **Walk the talk:** you are going to be competing for talent with large companies that have deep pockets, and you can't afford to pay what they do, so you get employees by making clear that you will only hire the best; and believe me, they will know if your newbie isn't up to snuff. If you tolerate it, you are sending the wrong message to the rest of the staff.

3. **How to handle mistakes:** as mentioned earlier, I am convinced that one of the keys to building a successful start-up is giving people room to take risks and make mistakes—great things are not accomplished without risk. A bad hire gives you the chance to let people know that it's OK to screw up once in a while; the important thing is that you acknowledge the mistake and move swiftly to correct it. How you handle your own mistakes will do much more to convey this message than covering the walls with motivational posters. I'm not saying you should go out and hire a total loser just to prove this point, but once you've made the mistake, you might as well at least polish the turd to its highest gloss.

Let's spend a little time talking about how to get the great employees you need and what you should and should not be prepared to offer to get them. First of all, what shouldn't you do? Remember the old days before you started your own company and you were a mid-level manager for Intel? Now imagine that you are interviewing for a software engineer position, and you're wrapping up an interview with a candidate who looks pretty good, and you start talking about the compensation package—salary, insurance, retirement, and so on. The interviewee tells you that it all sounds fine, but what he's really interested in is how much of the company he's going to get. After you finish laughing, you suddenly realize that he's serious and thinks he should get a percentage of the company for signing on. Of course, you politely thank him for his time and send him on his way.

Unfortunately, the media is full of stories about companies doing IPOs for billions of dollars and making instant multimillionaires of early employees who cashed in their options and never have to work again. This has created the notion that an equity piece is part of any compensation package for a start-up, and it may come as quite a shock when you don't put this on the table right away. Given the number of times in this book that I have mentioned the importance of cash flow and conserving cash, you may wonder why I don't endorse giving up some equity to get an employee to take less cash in exchange for some shares. After all, equity has a number of appealing qualities: it saves cash, it gives employees a set of goals in common with yours, and the only way it has any value is if the company is successful and you are either making a boatload of money or have a liquidity event. All true, but remember also that I have compared giving up equity to getting married—it's easy to do, but it can be really hard to undo later if you decide that it isn't working out. And yes, I know that you can design equity plans with options and vesting and other triggers that can minimize the negative impact, and I'm not saying that you should never do it—just be sure that you only put equity on the table when it is really necessary to get an employee who is really critical to the overall success and are not just handing it out like Halloween candy.

One way around giving out equity is to provide employees with the option to earn profits interests. The details of profits interests are beyond our scope, but suffice to say that they can provide a way to let employees participate in the success of the company after they have proven their value. The employer (and partners) benefits because the value of any profits interests are based on value added after they are awarded, meaning that the people who took the most risk early on don't have to give up that value but only any additional value that employees add. The employee can benefit because profits interests have no value when they are awarded, so there is no tax hit from awarding stock with a high valuation that is taxed as short-term gains—just look in to it and see if it fits with your needs.

So how do you compete for the people you really want without giving away the store? First remember that you have a number of advantages for someone looking to break out from the typical corporate grind:

- **Environment:** There is a very unique feeling to a start-up that can't be replicated in a big company, especially if you have some traction in the market.
- **Challenge:** The kind of people you want in your company aren't the "make the doughnuts" kind of employees who just want to punch the clock and get paid for what they do; they want to challenge themselves and prove what they can do.
- **Opportunity:** Any high-growth start-up provides unique opportunities for personal growth and development as well as advancement. A company that is doubling in size every year provides employees with the chance to take on new responsibilities and jobs.
- **Flexibility:** Being the boss means that you can be flexible in compensation, hours, and benefits to the extent money allows. My companies always provided monthly bonuses to every employee in the company based on how well the company performed to plan. Large companies can't do this, and it gives

you the ability to provide attractive near-term rewards if the company succeeds.

- **Upside:** I mentioned profits interests earlier, and whether you use profits interests or options or whatever, I think it is a great idea to make some form of ownership available to employees who have proven themselves over time—just don't give it away on the front end to someone who has not shown value. Make sure that you have a formalized program in writing that you can provide to potential employees as part of a hiring package so both parties understand the intent and mechanisms.

So what kind of employees are you looking for? In my experience, I prefer to go after people who have high potential and the right attitude over experience. This doesn't mean that I don't value experience and a solid résumé, but I have had great success hiring people with less experience for many jobs (sales, engineering, and production) if they had the right fundamentals and enthusiasm. For one thing, people with less experience will probably cost less; and although in some cases you get what you pay for, I'd much rather have someone who is willing to learn than someone who already knows it all. Another advantage is that you don't have to break old habits about how to do things. Presumably you are breaking new ground with your products, and employees with years of experience with how things are done may find it difficult to adapt. You are going to encourage your team to break the mold and take risks, and many people with a long time in the corporate world may be challenged to deliver what you want. Finally (and maybe most importantly), if you let potential hires know that you are taking a chance with them, they are far more likely to remain loyal when times get tough or when competitors come calling down the road. We'll deal a lot more with the attributes of employees for specific positions, but the main thing to keep in mind is to not compromise on quality—find the best and figure out how to get them onboard.

Suppliers

For many of you, it may seem strange to include suppliers in the list of people you work with; after all, you just buy stuff from them and they supply it, right? If you're talking about office supplies or other commodities, you may be right, but in all likelihood you will find that there are certain goods and services that you need that are absolutely critical to the success of the company, and you want to build relationships with suppliers that you can trust. Note that I said relationships as these critical suppliers are really more partners than vendors, and they need to understand what your expectations and needs are and their willingness to work with you is far more important than getting the cheapest price over the long haul. In a high-growth environment you are likely to need flexibility and cooperation from key suppliers to meet your needs. If you have a critical order from a customer on a tight schedule, you want to know that the contract manufacturers building your boards will do everything they can to help you meet the deadline.

Keep in mind that a critical supplier is any supplier who can shut you down or delay your production. My companies both manufactured electronic devices and used a number of electronic components ranging from resistors to ARM 9 processors (and pretty much everything in between). While virtually all of these components were readily available on the market from a variety of suppliers, many were subject to occasional and unpredictable shortages due to high demand in the market or production delays, and almost all of them were subject to end-of-life calls, which meant that the manufacturer was going to cease production of a particular product at a certain time in the future. In some cases, the manufacturer provided a replacement that was perfectly acceptable, but other times the replacement product had different specs or tolerances that would require modifications to other components to work. Under normal circumstances, these parts would be considered commodities, as they were available from multiple sources, but working with a good distributor could be the difference between meeting order commitments and shutting down for a period of time;

to me, our supplier and our relationship with the supplier was critical. As an example, if we had a part that was subject to high variability of supply, our supplier would buy and hold extra parts as a cushion in case our needs changed or there were interruptions in the supply chain.

We also had a few custom components that were critical to our production, primarily custom housings that required the production of very large, expensive tools to go in plastic injection molding machines. The tools were very complex, custom-made steel tools that were put into very large machines and injected with liquid plastic under intense heat and pressure. There are a number of injection molding companies and tooling makers, but we worked with the same plastics manufacture for over twenty years. I imagine we could have saved a few dollars by shopping with multiple suppliers, but we had a very good working relationship with our supplier—on several occasions we requested an unscheduled change to production because we had underestimated our needs. This is a very costly and time-consuming process, as inserting the tool into the press requires a crane and several hours of setup time, but in almost every case the supplier worked closely with us to provide as much help as possible. The value of this cooperation can't be overestimated and is worth paying a few extra dollars here and there.

Customers

I have to assume that you have experience (or someone on your team does) in working with customers, so I'm not going to spend a lot of time on the basics of relating to customers. Our focus will be on what is different about owning your own company and dealing with some of the customer issues you should be aware of. If you're not aware of the eighty/twenty rule, it is essentially that in a small company, 80 percent of your business will come from 20 percent of your customers; and in my experience, it's actually pretty accurate. Obviously this will be different if you are running Facebook or some other social media site that has millions of customers, but if you are working in a B2B industry, you will likely be surprised at how close this ratio is. There is another eighty/twenty rule that you should be aware of as a small business owner: 20 percent of your customers will consume 80 percent of your time and resources. This is fine if the same 20 percent of your customers are buying 80 percent of your products and using 80 percent of your resources, but this is often not the case, and this is when you may have to step in and fire some of your customers. On many occasions throughout the years, I have found salespeople, engineers, production employees, and finance personnel spending a great deal of their time working on issues related to customers who bought very small amounts. Sometimes you will have customers who feel that their needs are the highest priorities and place inordinate demands for delivery, pricing, specifications, and so on; and the "customer comes first" mentality you have ingrained in your employees can bite you in the ass. I've had to fire customers on several occasions over the years and it is just as painful as it sounds; but if someone continually eats a huge chunk of scarce resources, you may have to tell them that you will no longer be able to work with them. Not a decision to take lightly, given how hard you will have to work to get these customers, but you are the only one who can make the call; so bite the bullet and get it over with.

One of the happiest times of your start-up life will be the day when you finally land that big customer who is going to provide you with large purchase orders, access to new channels, and instant credibility in the market. One of the most miserable times of your start-up life will be when you look at the terms that large customer will accept. Most of your customers will happily accept your standard 1/10 net 30 terms (translation: 1 percent discount if paid within ten days, otherwise due in thirty days), but large companies know that they are bringing you large purchase orders and that you will probably cave and agree not only to 2 percent discount in fifteen days but also net forty-five (or sixty or even ninety days). Remember that scene in *Animal House* where Kevin Bacon is getting paddled as part of his fraternity initiation? "Thank you, sir; may I please have another?"

It's pretty much like that, but there is a bright side once you figure how big companies work. In my industry, people in engineering and operations made the decisions regarding what to buy, and the terms were set by the accounting folks. Oddly enough, these two groups were almost always working under different incentives—the engineers needed to buy the best products for their projects to make money and produce happy customers while the finance people were incented to preserve the company's cash. Once I figured this out, the answer was simple: I wasn't going to change the terms, so I had to float the cash myself; and this can be expensive, so I increased the price of the products I quoted to recover the finance cost. The field people didn't care as the amount of the increase was minimal, and they were getting the best products; and the finance people were happy because they got their terms. Everybody was happy.

I have another favorite saying that small business owners should take to heart: if you have a single customer who represents 25 percent of your sales or more, you no longer have a customer, you have a partner. Think about it.

Shareholders

Unless you have experience owning or managing a small company, you have likely never had to deal with fellow shareholders. The good news is that the rules are simple: the majority shareholder makes the rules. Period. End of story. Thanks for playing. Have a nice day.

If you are the majority shareholder, this seems like a great deal; and for the most part, it certainly is, but remember that this authority also brings responsibility. Even though you have all the clout, you need to keep in mind that abusing that position can easily cost you valuable employees; and you have an obligation to do the right thing by your fellow shareholders and not be a dick. This is absolutely one of those cases where you can win battles and still lose the war, but this is also why you have to be very careful to make sure as the founder of a start-up that you keep your hard-earned majority stake and give away only as much as you have to.

If you are the minority shareholder, you need to understand that math is a cruel mistress; and as our friend Dave discovered, 60 percent is always more than 40 percent, unless you are operating in some alternate universe that I'm not aware of. You may have heard of the golden parachutes that some executives get, but minority shareholding comes with a pair of golden handcuffs—you don't have control over your destiny, and leaving, as a matter of principle, typically comes with a high price. Your shares have little or no value on the market until the majority shareholder decides to sell, and you really don't have any say in that, either—if he or she decides to sell, you are likely going along for the ride. If you are not very good friends with the majority shareholder, you'd better hope that he or she is a benevolent dictator; otherwise, you are totally rolling the dice.

One question that arises occasionally is how to figure out the equity split on the front end of the start-up. The short answer is that if you're all bringing cash, it's simple; but if you are doing anything else, it's tough. Another complication is that you will negotiate the split on the front end based on contributions, but you should also address the issue of additional capital, which will almost certainly be required. Let's look at a fictitious example. One partner brings $20,000 in cash, another has $10,000, and the third has some software that he has written that will greatly facilitate the development of the product. If it's just the two guys with money, that's no problem, as the split is 66 percent/33 percent—but how do you figure the value of the software (or any other service or tools or whatever that is not cash)? If possible, you should try to establish a dollar value for the software (and by the way, you need this anyway for when you sell for millions and need to have a basis value). This is somewhat easier if the software has some value outside of the company, as it could theoretically be sold if the company goes belly up and the money split between the partners; however, this is unlikely, so you kind of have to play it by ear. The logical place to start is to put the burden on the developer to come up with a value and provide whatever justification he or she can bring to back up the valuation and negotiate from there. Wish there was a better answer, but there just isn't—it's a very tough negotiation, but you have to have it—and document it when you're done. If you want to add the complexity of who's going to do what work, it gets even crazier. Unless all three of you are going to work full time on the project, you may have one partner who promises to work more hours in exchange for equity, and that's a real sticky mess. Good luck with that.

Don't pat yourself on the back for having done the initial discussion and split, because you will almost certainly need more cash as time goes on, and now is the time to reach an agreement on that. It is unlikely that partners will be able to continue to contribute equally, and you have to arrive at a value for each dollar contributed after the initial round. One way I have done this in the past was to go back to the business plan and figure out the total cash commitment to positive cash flow and work from there. For example, if you figured you needed a total of $250,000, then each $25,000 would be worth 10 percent of the company; so each $25,000 contribution would be worth 10 percent of the shares authorized, not counting what has already been contributed. This sounds really complicated (and it is), so let's see if we can come up with an example. Let's say that one partner has contributed $75,000 and the other $25,000, so the initial split is seventy-five/twenty-five, and the company needs an additional $25,000. If the larger partner puts in all $25,000, the split would now be eighty/twenty (and if all the additional capital up to $250,000 came from the same partner, the final split would be ninety/ten—if this seems confusing, just remember that the smaller partner has contributed $25,000, or 10 percent of the total contributed capital). This is a good time to remind you that the majority shareholder has a responsibility to the minority partners to do the right thing. I had a similar agreement at one of my companies, but I chose to treat the cash as loans to the company rather than invested capital because it seemed like the fair thing to do, the cash was needed for a fairly short term and most importantly my partner was contributing long hours and adding far more value to the company than my cash.

One other thing: please keep in mind that people change when there is money involved, and you may have a very good working relationship through several years of partnership and find that things become very different when you are close to the endgame and cashing out. People who have told you that they will take care of you once the company sells will become incredibly greedy when there are millions on the table. If you are the majority shareholder, put yourself in the minority holders' shoes and be as fair as you possibly can and still come away with what you want. Karma's a bitch.

I'm not bragging when I say that I structured the sale of my last company so that minority shareholders were well taken of (to the extent that it cost me well north of a million dollars out of pocket), and I would do it again in a heartbeat. I came out fine, and I can honestly say that any of those folks would sign up again to do another company with me without hesitation—and that is worth every penny.

Now that we've talked about people in general, let's take a look at how to manage different departments and the wayward souls who populate them.

8

SALES

I've already mentioned my bachelor's degree in marketing, but I should probably also disclose that I got my start in business as a sales rep for Honeywell Homes and Buildings Group in Portland. I was promoted to sales manager for the branch and eventually branch manager before starting my first company. Over the years I have probably had at least fifty people work for me in a variety of sales roles, and I have built sales departments from scratch at both of my start-ups, so I feel very qualified to discuss the good and bad of working with and managing sales departments and people.

I want to begin by addressing the stereotype that sales people are arrogant, overpaid, underworked individuals who require constant care and attention. For the most part this is true, and quite frankly the best sales reps are those who are a little cocky. If they're paid a great deal of money, that's great, as long as they are producing sales. Sales are the engine of the company, and they provide the income that pays for everybody else in the company—if you don't have good sales reps, your company won't grow. With regard to money, I once heard a very good line from another manager whose comment was, "Salespeople are coin-operated: as long as you keep putting money in the slot, you will get what you want." Generally speaking, you want to hire reps who are constantly in debt—in fact, I always did a private happy dance whenever a rep would pull into the parking lot driving a shiny new car two days after getting a big incentive check because I knew he or she had just taken on a lot of debt and would be highly incented to keep the money flowing in. Fiscal responsibility should not be high on the attribute list when you are hiring.

Before I get into too much detail about finding and hiring reps, let's step back and talk about some of the fundamentals you need to know about building a sales strategy and program. For those readers who have a great deal of experience in sales and marketing, you can skip this part, but keep in mind that, as with most things, there are significant differences with a small company that might be useful to know, so humor me and at least skim through it.

One of the things that I hear often from entrepreneurs with technical backgrounds is, "Why should I spend time on sales planning now? If I don't get this product done, we don't have anything to sell, so it's completely irrelevant." What this tells me is that the person has failed to grasp the difference between being an engineer (or engineering manager) and an entrepreneur. As the owner of the company, you wear all the hats—CEO, CFO, CTO, COO, and probably janitor—and you don't have the luxury of focusing on one piece of the puzzle to the exclusion of others. If you've learned anything from this book, it should be that your focus is not on having a completed product as soon as possible but on being ready to build, sell, ship, and invoice for that product. Yes, you have to have a finished product, but if you leave all the other details till it's ready, your company will struggle and likely fail. You need to have a lot of balls in the air at one time and have multiple activities and plans running concurrently, not consecutively, or you will add months to the critical time of turning a project into a business.

Does this mean you shouldn't spend most of your time on product development? Of course not. First of all, you should have done at least some of the rudimentary planning for your sales strategy when you built your business plan, and hopefully all you really need to do is make any necessary tweaks to that bare-bones plan, begin figuring out what the tasks are, and filling in dates and details. I'm also not saying that you should rush out and hire a sales team six months before your product will be ready and have them sit around and play solitaire on your nickel. One of the nice things about strategy is that it doesn't involve stopping your code work every day at 10:00 a.m. and spending two hours typing your sales strategy. You need to work out your plan in your head before you put it on paper, and the best time to mull things over is when you are not sitting at your desk—I've always found it difficult to do creative work on a timeline or schedule. Some of the best ideas I've ever had have come to me when I was out running or driving to a relative's house for dinner or hiking in the woods. Your mind can wander, and you don't generally have a lot of distractions to interrupt your train of thought. By the time you get around to putting any of your ideas on paper, you should have a very good idea about where you are going, and it's just a matter of putting those ideas into an action plan. One of the most dangerous traps for founders to get caught in is falling back on doing the things you understand and are most comfortable with. Sometimes the most valuable thing you can do is get out of your comfort zone and tackle things that aren't in your wheelhouse.

The really good news for those of you with little or no experience in sales and marketing is that any good plan is built around a few simple concepts (it's the details and implementation that provide the real challenges). The first thing to remember is to keep everything as simple as possible: products that are easy to use, messages that are easy to understand, and a minimum of layers between you and your customers. As I often tell people, I was a "C" student through all my years in education, and I get headaches and nosebleeds when dealing with complex issues, so I work hard at reducing everything to the simplest terms possible. This is the single most important thing to remember when designing your sales and marketing strategy.

Any successful sales and marketing campaign at its heart is based around three attributes of your product:

- **Feature**—these are the descriptive attributes of your product, frequently technical in nature. For example, if you are building a microprocessor, one of the features is the clock speed of the chip (e.g., one GHz). Features are objective measures and subject to little or no interpretation.

- **Function**—this tells you what a particular feature performs or provides. In the example above, the function provided by a one-GHz processor speed is that it allows the chip to perform more instructions in a shorter period of time than other micros with slower clock speeds.
- **Benefit**—this is what the customer gains from the feature and its function (why should I buy this?). In our example above, a customer who buys a computer with a processor that is twice as fast as competitive models can get more work done in the same amount of time (cost savings). Keep in mind that there may be different benefits to different customers and others in the supply chain. In this case, the ultimate user may save money by saving labor, but the retailer may benefit from stocking only one model to meet the needs of multiple customers (reduced inventory costs).

You may think this is all intuitive, and the customer should be able to read a spec sheet and figure out for him- or herself what the functions and benefits are, but this is very rarely the case. If we look at the micro example, the end user may have no idea if one GHz is really fast (and probably doesn't care), so if you don't explain how it benefits him or her, he or she will likely buy a cheaper model with a slower processor. If you can quantify the benefits to the customer, he or she really doesn't care about the specs but rather cares about what the micro will do to benefit him (save money).

Thinking through the feature set of your product (and the associated functions and benefits) early in the process can be very valuable to you for several reasons:

1. Translating the key features in your products into the benefits they provide to the customer may lead you to add (or delete) features that you hadn't considered, particularly when you consider your product relative to competitive products.

2. Even if you don't add or delete features, you may find that you can prioritize the features by the benefit provided, which will allow you to address the most important features first and possibly even develop a phased product rollout where critical features are available immediately and lower priority features my be available down the road. As a side note, if the ability to upgrade the features in your product easily in the field isn't one of your features, you should probably think about it.

3. Like it or not, one of your many hats is chief salesperson. Customers (especially large customers) are not going to place large POs with small companies at trade shows from talking to sales reps in the booth. You, your company, and your products are basically inseparable, and you need to figure out how to sell your products yourself.

4. The features of your product may have a significant impact on your channel. Let's say that you're going into a market where competitive products are complex and expensive to set up and install. If one of the features of your product is that it is simple and can be installed by anyone, you may be able to build a sales channel that lets you sell directly to end users rather through distributors or contractors. What this means to you is that you can sell the product for the same price and keep the extra margin without paying any commissions or markups (see what I did there—turned a feature into a benefit for you, and I'll bet you understood it immediately. Marketing at its finest).

5. Even if you don't spend a minute in the booth or schmoozing customers (shame on you), you still need to be able to convey the benefits of your products in a simple, clear manner. First, you need to have your elevator speech ready for the time when you find yourself on a seventeen-floor journey with a large customer. Second, you will have to sell others (investors, bankers, suppliers) on why your company will be successful and they should work with you—even if they don't understand the technical aspects, they can see the benefits quite clearly.

Now that you're much more comfortable with your role of chief schmoozer, let's start taking a look some of the things you need to look at and plan for in building your sales and marketing strategy. As always, remember, this is not an exhaustive list or a formula for success but rather a way of looking at particular issues. Part of the joy and challenge of your new role is figuring these things out and coming up with creative ways of solving problems and growing your business.

Go to Market Strategy

I'm hoping that no one needs me to describe what "go to market strategy" means—it's probably the most self-explanatory phrase in this book (with the possible exception of "polishing a turd")—so let's get on with looking into the different aspects of your go-to-market plan with a primary focus on distribution and sales models. Keep in mind that all of the topics in this chapter are heavily interrelated, and changes to one aspect (e.g., distribution) can have a major impact on others (like pricing), and all the pieces should be consistent with each other and with your overall business philosophy.

I'm sure that you built a distribution strategy when you built your business plan, but let's be honest—you did a half-assed job and basically copied what your competitors are doing. And why wouldn't you? It's a proven channel that's already in place with customers and resellers who know the product and know where to find it. But think back to our discussion about product development. We didn't start with what competitors were doing and try to do it better; we started with what was the best thing for the customer and worked from there. If you don't think they got their products right, why would you think they did a great job with distribution and that you should just copy it? In the HVAC world, most products are sold by manufacturers' reps to distributors, then to contractors, and ultimately to homeowners. Nothing wrong with this, but before you chase this model (or any other), ask yourself a few questions and see if distribution presents potential competitive advantages.

The first question you should ask is this: what value does the current chain add to your products (not your competitors' products, but yours)? The HVAC distribution model was built a very long time ago, when communications and travel were difficult and expensive and products were complex with limited user interface for setup, so it made sense. The manufacturer sells to one rep, who sells to multiple distributors in geographic markets, who sell to multiple contractors in a local area, who each sell to many homeowners; so this model allowed a small manufacturer to gain instant distribution across the country very quickly and also allowed for larger sales to fewer customers (lowering sales and shipping costs). Let's have some fun with pretend numbers (as they are much easier than working hard to get real ones). Assume that a manufacturer builds a product for the HVAC market that costs fifty dollars to build, and he wants a 50 percent gross margin, so he needs to gross one hundred dollars for each unit. How does this affect the final price that the end user pays after going through the channel? Let's look:

- Price from manufacturer — $100.00
- Price with rep commission (5%) — $105.26
- Price with distributor markup (10%) — $116.95
- Price with contractor markup (20%) — $146.20

Seems reasonable, right? The customer pays around $150 for the product, and the manufacturer makes $50 gross margin so everybody wins. But what if the manufacturer could sell directly to the customer (say, by making a product that can be installed by the homeowner without the contractor and selling it on the Internet)? The manufacturer could sell the product directly and collect the $146.20, almost doubling his gross margin dollars and increasing his gross margin percentage from 50 percent to 66 percent ($96.20), or an extra $46.20 per unit. In fact, the manufacturer could probably charge even more because the homeowner wouldn't have to pay $100 to a contractor to do the installation (meaning that selling it at $250 would be a break-even for the homeowner). I'm not saying this is even possible, but if I were in this business, it is definitely something worth thinking about. Your biggest advantage as a small company is flexibility, and part of this flexibility is the opportunity to create new channels that can cut costs or provide more value to customers, so don't waste an opportunity to make a bunch more money and add value. Here are some of the most common go-to-market channels and their pros and cons:

- Manufacturer's reps—these are folks who do not buy your products and resell them but rather act as your representative in specific channels and markets for a percentage of the sales. The biggest plus to having reps is that you can get instant exposure to a number of potential buyers without-out-of pocket costs (reps are paid after the sale). The downside to reps is that many of them are just looking to fill out a line card (a list of products they represent), and they often have more products than they can handle and do a poor job of selling your products. Unless you can command a big percentage of their business, your stuff may simply be an afterthought or a reason for them to call a customer and not something that they are really interested in selling. You are also responsible for advertising and marketing costs and providing the rep with leads to follow up on. Costs vary, but you can plan on paying from 5 to 20 percent or more, depending on the products and markets.
- Distributors—these people actually buy your products for resale to others or to end users. The advantage to distributors is that you can make a few sales in large quantities and get distribution into a wide range of markets very quickly. The drawback to distributors is that they are historically poor at selling products, and their primary value is simply that they stock products locally that customers want to buy. In addition to bearing the cost of advertising and tech support, the manufacturer will also need to provide POS (no, not that POS—this one is point-of-sale) materials for the distributor to display. These guys will take a 10 percent minimum markup (and probably closer to 15 or 20 percent for a small company).

- Retailers—I never used them, so I hardly consider myself an expert. Obviously the key question here is whether you have a product that lends itself to retail sales and if so what kind of retailers you want to use. Just like any other channel, ask yourself if your product fits and what value is added—you're on your own here.

- Value added resellers (VARs)—you may not be familiar with VARs, so let me provide a little more background on them. These guys basically buy your product and either use it as part of a larger system or add other hardware or software to "customize" your product for a specific market or application. They may simply buy your product branded as is or repackage and/or rebrand it as their own. You may need to add custom features to your product for them, usually in exchange for volume purchase commitments or NRE (nonrecurring engineering) expense. The nice things about VARs are that they buy the product (and hopefully pay) and may allow you to get in to specialized markets without a lot of additional costs. This is another example of using marketing to build a feature set for your product—if you have potential for VAR customers, you should design your product to be easily customized for different applications and markets.

- Direct sales—just what it says, you sell your products directly to the end users without any middlemen. This option is gaining more popularity, largely because of a new fad called the Internet (I'm not sure it will last, but it might hang on long enough to at least consider) as it provides a vehicle not only for sales and advertising but payment as well. If you are starting any kind of company today and don't consider the impact of the web now and in the future, this would be a good time to slip in your favorite eight-track cassette and think again, 'cause your competitors (present and future) will. As we saw earlier, selling direct has a financial advantage, but it also has several other pluses: you know who you are selling to, you collect immediately, and you can gain a great deal of data about buying habits and patterns. The further you are removed from the end user, the harder it is for you to learn what works and what doesn't, so think hard about finding some way to control your own destiny.

- International distribution—I am aware that we live in a digitally connected world and have a global economy (hell, even Fox News sometimes slips up and says something positive about business outside the lower forty-eight), but I encourage great caution when approaching the international market (and this applies whether you are in the United States or not). If you think this advice applies only to makers of electrical or consumer products, just ask a couple of large social media companies if they are having any special challenges in countries like China or Turkey (see, I didn't even have to mention North Korea to make my point). Let's look at some of the challenges:

  o Regulatory—the same product that sails through UL in this country faces a whole new set of requirements to meet CE specifications for Europe and other parts of the world.
  o Language—not only do you have to sell in different languages, but all your marketing and installation materials and labels have to be translated as well. This may be pretty straightforward for many products, but if you make something that is highly technical and specialized, just finding someone to translate the material can be incredibly difficult.
  o Politics—many decisions outside your home country may be made for political rather than economic or technical reasons. Some countries want to protect domestic companies while others want to retain a level of control over content that may be impossible to overcome.
  o Legal—when you do business in another country, you are subject to their laws governing contracts, sales, and term. I learned this the hard way when I tried to fire a rep in another country. In the United States, you can generally terminate a rep with an agreement to pay commissions on any

sales in his territory for ninety days, but I discovered that if I terminated this rep, he would still receive commissions for five years on anything sold in that country. *Oops!*

o Exchange rates—about the only time most of us are aware of exchange rates is when we land in a foreign country at 3:00 a.m. after fifteen hours of flying and try to figure out whether 100,000 Shaquillies is $10 or $1,000. It's a little different if you are selling overseas; if you sell someone a product in Euros based on today's exchange rate, you need to realize that you will be paid in Euros a month or two down the road at whatever the exchange rate is on that date, so you can get burned. You can mitigate this by making sure that all quotes are in US dollars (the buyer takes the risk of fluctuation) and getting your money up front via wire transfer. While this does provide great protection, imagine if you ordered a part from London and had to pay in pounds sterling in advance—you'd have to want that part pretty badly as it's a pain in the ass. Same for your customers. And yes, you can hedge your currency exposure, but unless you are a big player, it isn't worth the trouble.

Pricing

You may think that pricing belongs in the financial section, but keep in mind that pricing is a critical part of your sales and marketing strategy. There are several models out there for pricing, and we'll get to those shortly; but anytime you approach pricing, there are a number of things to keep in mind. The first is that in the absence of other information, price equals perceived value. Imagine that you walk into a car dealership and see two similar cars next to each other, one with a sticker price of $30,000 and the other with a sticker price of $40,000. I don't know about you, but my first assumption is that the higher-priced vehicle has more features or options that make it more valuable to most buyers (this may not be true for all buyers, as different buyers have different tastes, but it can be assumed to be true for the average buyer). You may be tempted to put a low price on your product to gain market share (and cash flow), but this may cause customers to think that your product is inferior and not take the time to explore the features of the product. If you are building a product whose primary value is low price, this is great, but if you are selling a product superior to competitive products, you are sending an inconsistent message if the price is too low.

Note that there is no single right pricing model, just the right one for your product and company. Sam Walton was a big believer in "stack 'em deep and sell 'em cheap," and this is still the practice Walmart uses today in pricing. Even if you've never been in a Walmart, their advertising would lead you to expect that you can buy Cheerios cheaper at Walmart than anywhere else; and if that's important to you, then you know where to go to get it. On the other end of the scale, Bugatti proudly boasts that its Vayron is the most expensive sports car in the world at roughly $2.5 million per car. Clearly different philosophies, but Walmart is the largest retailer in the world, and Bugatti has a two-year waiting list, so both seem quite successful. Just be sure that the price you charge is consistent with the message you are delivering, and you'll be OK.

There are essentially two pricing models in wide use. The first is called cost-based pricing and essentially applies a desired margin to the cost of goods sold (COGS) to arrive at a market price. In our earlier example in the HVAC world, the company had a build cost of fifty dollars and a target gross margin of 50 percent, so the price would be one hundred dollars. Although this model is simple and provides an easy way to track performance, it has a significant flaw that you hopefully saw in our earlier example: that the market may well accept a much higher price, and you are leaving money on the table, particularly when a product is new and has significant advantages over existing competition. Also, if you stick to this model and manage to reduce your costs through lower pricing, do you reduce the selling price as well?

The best model, in my opinion, is a market-based model like we discussed earlier, where the same product could be sold with more margin for the company by eliminating middlemen. You can also charge more early on when the advantages are clear and move the price down when and if competitors respond with changes to their products without hurting your margin. The only danger to this strategy is that setting a high price creates a potential window of opportunity for competitors to copy your features and sell at a lower price and force you to respond. This is why you don't want to price your product at the absolute maximum you can; instead, find a price that meets or exceeds your gross margin needs without creating opportunities for competitors.

There are a couple of other things to keep in mind that may sound silly but actually have some basis in the psychology of buyers. The first is to price your product in a way that creates an impression of value—for example, $999 sounds a lot less than $1,000, even though the difference is only a buck. Laugh if you will, but it works. The other thing is to price products at odd prices, which gives the impression that you have developed a formula to calculate the price and implies that there is less room for negotiation. For instance, pricing a product at $1,000 might lead a customer to think you yanked a number out of your ass (which you did), but the same product priced at $994 sounds like it was carefully calculated (even though you used the same method to get to the price). Goofy, I know—but believe me, it works.

Trade Shows and Promotions

Most industries have at least one trade show each year, and in my experience, trade shows make for a love-hate relationship with start-ups. There are customers there—if you pick the right shows—and it can be a great way to meet a lot of new potential buyers, especially for a company that's new in the market and needs the exposure. On the other hand, unless the show is in your hometown, the cost of going to a trade show can be a budget buster. Here's a rough budget to send two people to your first trade show in another city:

- Booth and graphics — $10,000
- Booth rental — $7,500
- Miscellaneous electrical — $500
- Travel — $1,000
- Hotels — $1,500
- Meals — $1,000
- Entertainment — $1,000

Total — $22,500

If this seems like a lot of money, that's because it is—in fact, it's a small fortune for a start-up company, so you need to pick your trade shows carefully. In my companies, even though we were in a fairly specialized industry, there were probably ten or twelve shows we could do each year, which would cost a cool quarter of a million bucks. I'd love to tell you that there was an easy way to measure the value of a trade show, but unfortunately most of the new business you develop will take a while to turn into business, so you may need at least six months or more to figure out if it was a success in terms of new business.

We used trade shows primarily as a venue for meeting with existing customers to finalize deals and socialize, with a much lower emphasis on finding new customers. Using this approach meant that we could meet with multiple customers on one trip rather than traveling all over the country to see them, so it made sense that way. One key to making a trade show successful is to treat it as a sales call. In addition to the time spent in the booth, each attendee has several opportunities throughout the day to schedule meetings with customers (breakfast, coffee, lunch, beers, dinner, and after-dinner drinks), so if you sent two people for three days, you had six meeting times per day per rep for three days, thus a total of thirty-six potential meetings. Young salespeople think that going to trade shows is a real treat, as they get free airfare, nice hotels, meals, and bar tabs paid for; the deal was that they had to have a certain percentage of the available slots filled in advance, or they didn't go. You'd be amazed at how much more effective this was than leaving it to chance.

Website

Twenty-plus years ago, when I got the domain name for my first company and built the first website, a lot of people I knew asked some variation of the same question: Why are you spending money on that? And I have to confess that I didn't have a great answer. Only a handful of people were even using the web, and there certainly wasn't any way to see how it could be used to make money. I really did it for two reasons: (1) a couple of folks from my MBA program had started a company building websites, and they told me it was really cool, and I just had to do it (and they made me a deal if they could use my site for demos); and (2) there was this new-fangled thing called e-mail, and even though the only people I was e-mailing at the time were the guys who built the website, I was kind of fascinated with it. It's hard to imagine today just how primitive early websites were, but there really weren't many options—not only were there limited tools for building a site, but anyone who connected to it was doing so over a dial-up connection, and download speeds were measured in dozens of bits, not gigabytes. I think the most amazing thing to me is just how much of the infrastructure from the old days (domain names, URLs, hosting servers, etc.) is still the core of much of the functionality of the Web today. But enough time on memory lane—let's take a look at how the web fits into your business today.

The company website has gone from the gimmick of the 1990s to the primary face of your company today. Many of your customers will never visit your building or even talk to a human being in the company. They will handle all of their experience on the web; everything from product comparison to purchase to tech support will be handled via computer. This has a major impact on how you design your site and provides potentially

141

huge advantages—a twenty-four-hour sales department and tech support is just one example. If done properly, this means that you no longer have to worry about staffing for multiple time zones, and you can even have a storefront available to international customers on their schedules, regardless of where they are in the world. Pretty cool stuff.

I'm definitely not the guy to provide commentary on the state-of-the-art in web design and execution, as it is changing so quickly that you can't keep up and still have a life. Even so, I can provide some guiding principles to keep in mind. Before we get into the principles, pull out your business card and read your title. Unless it says "chief website developer" or something similar, read the next sentence very carefully. The cardinal rule of designing, building, and supporting your own website is this: don't design, build, or support your own website. And yes, I'm talking to all of you engineers and software geeks—I know that you are fully capable of building your own site and already have your own site that is vitally important for the sale and support of the handful of products you sell each year from that closetful of cool things that nobody knows about. Don't. Just don't. Why not? After all, you write code for a living, and why in the world should you spend money for something you can do for free? First of all, no offense, but the site you build will be technically outstanding and functional and also utterly worthless at selling your company and products. You know it's true, no matter how much it hurts. More importantly, building the website is not your job—your job is making sure that all the people who are doing all the disparate tasks needed to get you going are on the same page. Even if you are still the primary coder for the firmware in your products, this is a whole different deal, and you will suck at it. I won't dwell on this (you'll probably ignore me anyway), so let's take a look at some things you should keep in mind, whether you manage the website implementation or do it yourself:

- Consistency: Every time a customer experiences your company, he or she should see a consistent look, feel, and content. This applies to everything you produce, including print ads, data sheets, marketing materials, instruction manuals, booth graphics, e-mails, and (most importantly) the website. Even at a quick glance, anyone should be able to recognize that any materials (whether digital or printed) are from your company, and this applies to your site. Don't create new colors or logos or themes for the site—make sure that anything you do here is consistent with the rest of your message.

- Simplicity: Technology is a wonderful thing, but this is one of those times when you have to know the difference between "can" and "should." I know your developer has told you that he can have an anthropomorphic moose dance across the opening screen carrying your featured product of the month and singing the company jingle. And your customers may actually find it clever and intriguing—once. By the second time they have to see this (and waste fifteen or twenty seconds of their lives), they will be fidgety; by the third time, they will be muttering obscenities at the screen. By the fourth time...never mind; there won't be a fourth time.

- Standardization: Your first reaction to your first test of your sales module (select products, add to cart, view cart, go to checkout, select shipping, review order, add credit card info, push purchase button, don't press "back" or refresh, yada yada) might leave you disappointed. Your purchase process is just like everybody else's. Good! Now move onto something else, because this is just what you want. Your customers are dealing with a process that is years old and looks very similar, and this is perfect. They want to see the "Purchase" button in the lower right-hand corner and don't want to have to search for it. Resist the temptation to put a flashing red button in the screen labeled "Click here to begin the greatest purchase experience of your life and join thousands of other happy customers!" Give them the frigging purchase button and make the purchase process as easy as possible.

- Flexibility: You may be thrilled with the website today, but it's a given that you will want and need to make changes as time goes on. There will be new products, news updates, special offers, and so on, and you want to make sure of a couple of things: you need to know that changes can be made to the site easily and without altering the look and feel, and you don't want to have to go back to the web designer every time you need to make a change. This requires designing the site with modules that you can change yourself in a few minutes and not muck everything up. Very doable and an absolute must.

- Scalability: You are going to be growing this hot new company at a terrific pace, and the last thing you want is to have your website crash or cause your customers delays. This means that you need to address the volume of traffic the site can handle, both from a design perspective and in terms of the size of the pipeline that feeds the site. Either can cripple you, and you don't want to scramble for a fix.
- Quality: In addition to the consistency and appearance of your site, you need to pay close attention to the quality. You or someone on your staff needs to read every word and test every link to make sure there are no spelling or grammatical errors and that everything works. This is especially important when you are launching the site and when you make any changes. Stress-test every aspect of the site and make repairs your highest priority.

At the risk of pushing my personal preferences on you, I strongly encourage you to handle your sales directly through a combination of your website and the sales reps you hire. I realize how tempting it is for a start-up to use manufacturers' reps—no upfront costs and instant exposure to widely dispersed markets—but think hard before you go this route. Hiring your own reps gives you two big advantages: you can manage the activities of your reps very closely and know what progress is being made, and (most important) you can customize your incentive program to meet the short- and long-term needs of the company. Want to offer a bonus for sales of new products? No problem. Want to add a spiff for bringing in new customers in a particular market? Done. If you work with manufacturers' reps, you will have little control over their sales activities and will also have to accept industry standard terms, as they will not likely make changes to their terms and conditions for a start-up company with no market share.

So where do you find good reps? Well, you could do the usual route and look for experienced reps on websites or from competitors or search firms, but if you've followed my earlier advice and simplified your product and message, you don't really need people with lots of experience or technical knowledge (in fact, it may be a disadvantage). The primary characteristics you are looking for are reasonable intelligence, effective communication, and a focus on customer service. Where do you find them? How about the clerk in the men's department at Macy's who took the time to find out that you needed a suit for your sister's wedding but probably would rarely wear it afterward? She steered you to a midrange suit that would look just as good as high-end ones but wouldn't be as durable for everyday wear, even though she made less commission. Perfect. Or how about the waiter at Olive Garden who bent the rules a little bit and let you sample three wines instead of two to make sure you got what you wanted and asked about your tolerance for spice in helping you pick out an entrée? Yep. What about the guy at Jiffy Lube who showed you the engine air filter that looked dirty, but then fanned it out and explained that most of the dirt was on the surface and you could wait till next time? Yes, he missed the chance to sell you an incredibly marked-up filter, but the odds are that he created a long-term customer, and you need as many of those as you can get.

It goes without saying that with all the permutations and different ways to attack sales and marketing, we could go on forever, but at this point I'm sure everyone is dying to hear how our buddy Dave (anal retentive engineer) is dealing with the voodoo and mysticism surrounding sales and marketing. As you may recall, when we last left Dave, he had just learned the sheer joy of being a minority shareholder working with a majority shareholder whose idea of cutting back is ordering the American Wagyu burger and forgoing the much better Japanese Kobe beef burger at Callahan's Steak House. As you can imagine, it has not all been a bed of roses, but let's fast-forward ten months. Dave has busted his butt and completed the first of two prototypes he has promised to have ready for a contractors' trade show a month later in Chicago. To celebrate, he and Maggie are out to dinner with their accountant Mark and his wife. After the usual pleasantries and a couple of glasses of house chardonnay, the conversation turns to the business.

Mark says, "I gotta believe you've been burning the midnight oil—haven't seen you on the course in months."

"Yeah, it's been a little crazy, but at least the proto is done," says Mark.

"That's gotta be a great relief. You pretty jazzed?"

"Mostly excited and anxious to get it out there, but I have to admit I'm not sleeping well worrying that they might hate it or something could go wrong and it doesn't work."

"I hear you, but it's still damned impressive that you got this done in just ten months, especially with the issues you've had with your partner."

Somehow Mark manages to miss the grimace on Maggie's face and the slashing motion across her neck to try and steer clear of the subject, but to her surprise she doesn't get the explosion she has anticipated from her husband, and his response is surprisingly measured. "Well, you all know that I've had some real challenges with my little buddy, but I actually think I've made some real progress lately."

Maggie exclaims, "Well, that's news to me; all I've heard is a string of complaints. Do you mean that you've gotten him to work normal hours?"

"Oh, hell no! But I have figured out how to get the maximum out of the few hours he is willing to part with in his busy schedule."

"I'm starting to feel a bit like Alice chasing a white rabbit down a hole, but OK, what are you talking about?" asks Mark.

"Maggie's heard this a hundred times, but Mark and Kay, for your benefit, let me give you a little backstory. One of my pet peeves is people who use anecdotal evidence to make conclusions about things that could be easily quantified and used more effectively. Let me give you an example. If I told you that buildings use more air conditioning when the temperature is higher, would you be surprised?"

"Of course not."

"Right, but how do you know if the building is using more energy than it should? This is one of the key algorithms I've written into the EnerTroll. ET looks at the operation of the building and measures how much energy the building uses at different outside temps. It makes adjustments to schedules and set points based not only on building performance but also on weather data downloaded from NOAA weather websites. It builds a profile from historical info and then looks at day-ahead weather forecasts from NOAA to predict energy usage and makes adjustments based on how the building actually performs. Basically, it's searching for patterns of correlation between performance and weather data and using that data to predict the future performance of the building."

"Um, cool," says Mark.

Maggie takes over. "Don't worry, Mark. I've heard this same speech more times than I can count, and I still have no idea what he's talking about. The mystery to me is what this can possibly have to do with your favorite partner's work habits."

"Here's the thing," says Dave. "You know me, and I needed to quantify his hours and use that data to predict how much he would be working, so I started logging his arrival and departure times minus the time spent at lunch. Turns out our boy was putting in a grueling twenty-two and an half hours each and every week on average, but the problem was that there was a lot of variance from week to week. The only correlation I found was that Fridays and Mondays were high probability for absence."

"Hardly shocking news. So you had your data, and then what?"

"Yes, but not all that useful. If I needed something from Rick, I needed a reliable way to predict when he would be in the office, and that's when it hit me. What I was looking for was a way to predict a schedule based on correlation to outside factors—just what ET was designed to do," says Dave.

"So you used valuable time and resources to make your product predict when your partner would be in the office. How much time did that take?"

"That's the great part. I figured I would have to put in a whole bunch of new factors, but I decided to test the process by plugging his schedule into the system to correlate to the weather data ET was already getting, and boom! Turned out there was a high R-squared correlation between Rick's work hours and the temperature and solar index—actually, a negative correlation, since it really turned out that the warmer and sunnier the temperature, the less likely the princeling was to be in the office."

"And that helps how?" asks Mark.

"Simple. ET downloads the next week's forecast, and I can get a really good idea of when I have the best chance of getting some work out of him."

Maggie is more than a little troubled by the smug look on Dave's face and the twisted logic that he is so satisfied with what he's done. Still, he's more pleasant to be around than he had been in months, so what the heck.

Monday rolls around, and for once Dave is actually looking forward to seeing Rick (even though it's Monday, it's raining like crazy, and the model has a 90 percent or higher confidence level that Rick will show up at some point). Dave has spent most of the weekend putting finishing touches on the proto, and he can't wait to see Rick's face.

As predicted, Rick shows up at the crack of ten thirty, and after giving him an hour to update his Facebook page and download e-mails, Dave casually strolls over to Rick's desk with his hands behind his back.

"Hey, what's up? How was the weekend, Dave?" says Rick.

"Actually, pretty busy, since I spent most of it finishing this off." He hands Rick the prototype with an expectant grin on his face.

"I thought it was going to have a pebble finish. What happened?" asks Rick.

"Well, the injection molded product will have a pebble finish, but this one was made by a guy I know on a CNC machine, and I think it looks pretty good for a first pass. It will work great for the trade show next month," Dave tells him.

"I mean, it looks OK, I guess, but why didn't you just have it done at the injection molding house like we discussed?"

"We talked about this months ago, and we agreed that we would build the first few units this way to get customer feedback. Doing the tooling will cost seventy-five grand and take four months or more, and we didn't even have the final dimensions till a couple of weeks ago."

"How come we were so far behind on the final dimensions? Who f'ed that up?" demands Rick.

"If you go back to the development schedule on the back wall, you'll see that we are actually ahead of schedule by almost a week. And besides, we don't have seventy-five grand to tie up right now, so we couldn't do it anyway."

"Here we go again. I keep telling you to stop nickel and diming everything—we've got to start acting like a real company."

"Whatever. It doesn't matter now, since we're out of options. The good news is that you've got one prototype now, and I'll have another by the end of the week, so you'll have two for the trade show. You making any progress on hiring the reps before the show?"

"Oh yeah. Good news on that front—I ran into a frat brother of mine last week, and he will be perfect for the job."

"What's his degree in?" asks Dave.

"Oh, he only lasted for two terms, but he's a sharp guy and really fun to hang out with, so he'll be perfect," says Rick.

"And the other spot?"

"Done. My frat brother Barry has a buddy from the gym that he says will be perfect, and they are both starting next week."

"Does that give you enough time for training before you take them to the show?"

"No problem. Where is the show?"

"Chicago."

"I hate Chicago in the winter, and besides, I've been thinking that it would be better for you to go anyway. Be better for the guys and the customers if we have somebody there with more technical knowledge to answer questions," says Rick.

"So you're in charge of sales, but you're not going to our first trade show?" asks Dave incredulously.

"Ten-four. But wait till you see the shirts I've ordered—they're awesome, and the graphics and literature for the booth look great. Be good for you to get out and see some customers anyway."

"Correct me if I'm wrong, but if I see one customer, it will be one more than you've seen."

"True, but how could I go see customers with no product to show them? Was I supposed to do shadow puppets on the wall? I'd have been all over it if I had something to show, and that sounds like an engineering problem, so…"

"Never mind. And you're welcome." Dave just walks away.

Fast forward a few more weeks, and Dave is standing in the lobby of a Sheraton Hotel outside of Chicago at 3:30 a.m. To save money he had booked the flights for himself and Barry and Joe with a 5:30 a.m. departure with two stops. Add in almost five hours of weather delays on airplanes with nothing but peanuts and pretzels, and Dave was hard-pressed to figure out which was more important—food or sleep. The gym rats had voted for food, and after checking with the desk clerk, Dave had discovered that the only option was a Denny's open twenty-four hours just down the road, and they had dumped their bags in their rooms so they could get to the restaurant. Then the following conversation occurred.

Dave: "OK, let's get rolling. I'm starved."

Barry: "Wait a minute, we can't go yet."

Dave: "What? Why not?"

Barry: "I just got a look at myself in the mirror over there, and I definitely have to fix my hair."

Dave: "Are you out your mind? I've been up for close to twenty-two hours, and my last decent meal was breakfast. And besides, your hair looks just fine. And who the hell do you think you're going to impress at Denny's at four o'clock in the morning?"

Barry: "You never know, and I'm not taking any chances. Only problem is I don't have any hair gel. I figured we'd get here at a decent hour, and I'd be able to pick some up. Joe, you got any gel?"

Joe: "Yeah, let's go up to my room and get it taken care of."

Dave: "I've got the keys, and I'm leaving."

Barry: "C'mon, man. There might be some hot ladies over there, and we can probably get you hooked up if things work out. It'll only take a few minutes."

As Dave sits fuming on a couch in the lobby, he reminds himself that this is a small deal, and after all, things are going pretty well. Rick's gym rat buddies (or Hans und Franz, as he prefers to think of them) have actually turned out to be pretty good at what they do. Neither of them is likely to cure cancer or come up with the grand unified theory in physics, but give them a phone, a script, and a list of contractors, and they'll spend hour after hour making cold calls. Dave is actually very impressed that they can deal with all the rejections (they even have some sort of contest for the most innovative rejection with extra points for no swearing). Dave can't let them get far off script, as they do have a tendency to make up answers they don't know, but in the last two weeks they've somehow managed to get promises from two dozen contractors to stop by the booth during the show. They have to turn sideways to get their egos in the door, and the break area is filled with Costco-size tubs of protein powder and who knows what else, but they work eight- to ten-hour days and are making some real headway.

Despite his limited productive office time, Rick has actually managed to put together some pretty good marketing materials. The booth and graphics look sharp, the data sheets are really sharp, and he's even managed to produce a demo video that shows how easy the EnerTroll is to install and the great savings people can expect (of course, all the data is from the unit at Dave's house, and Dave had tweaked the calculations to accelerate the learning process, but it still looks really good). All of this has, of course, come at a price, as Rick did nothing himself and farmed it out to a former girlfriend who runs her own marketing company. So far, the costs have been triple what they'd agreed on, but they really are starting to look like a real company, and it feels pretty good. And there was the last minute scramble to get Hans und Franz new cell phones that were dedicated to the calls being forwarded from the office, as Rick isn't planning to be in the office much, but overall life is good, and Dave is optimistic.

Half an hour later, the boys return. Barry has taken the time to shower, and Dave is wishing he'd left, but he doesn't want to start the week that way.

Four days later, Dave is finally in a seat on a redeye flight back, feeling exhausted but fired up. Response to the ET was better than he could have hoped, and despite one of the prototypes crapping out in the middle of a demo for one of the largest contractors in the country, things had gone very well, with a couple of minor babysitting issues. The logoed shirts Rick had ordered looked sharp except for the fact that Barry and Joe both appeared to be wearing ladies' mediums, stretched to the point that the logo was almost unreadable. "Gotta let the babes check out the guns" was the explanation Dave got, and he decided that he had bigger fish to fry and let it go. The other minor problem was that one of the nearby booths was, to all appearances, staffed by young ladies who all would be pulling the late shift at Hooters (and wearing logo gear made from the same people who made their evening uniforms), and Dave found that he would frequently have to stop by that booth to retrieve the children and drag them back to the booth. All in all, Dave's first experience with marketing and trade shows went pretty well, and he is really fired up to get back to the office.

9

ENGINEERING

"**F**ire up the blender!"

I know I've spent a lot of time on the downside of giving away equity without a lot of thought, and I hope you are paying attention to that, but there is another side of the partner coin that deserves equal attention. When you do find the right partner(s), and both (or all) of you are fully committed and dependent on the company's success, there is no relationship in business that can compare. You have to have complete faith and trust in your cofounder and know that he or she will work just as hard as you do to make sure the company is a success. You will spend a lot of time together, and much of what gets accomplished is done with a minimum of communication. With the right partner, there is little need for discussion; when a product needs to get built and released, each of you understands that the other will complete his or her part to make everything work. Part of this relationship involves learning to speak in codes and catchphrases that others will never understand.

When I was looking around for someone to help me get my last company off the ground, I desperately needed someone who could provide the technical development skills that I knew I didn't have. I also knew that I needed a different type of engineer than those I had worked with at my first company as the focus here would be very much on software. This was unlike my first company, which was primarily a hardware provider with limited software requirements, so I didn't have a lot of good resources to fall back on. Fortunately, I did have one person who was not technically an employee of the company but provided network support for us and had a unique set of software and hardware skills that were a great fit for the product I had in mind. After a few months of contract work together, I knew that he was just the guy I needed. He not only possessed the technical skills I needed but also showed a remarkable patience for listening to many of my crazy ideas. So he became my CTO and cofounder.

The "Fire up the blender" phrase came from morning meetings he and I would have just about every day. They usually consisted of me wandering down to his office with a cup of coffee and settling into a big comfy chair that he had. After the usual banter, we would use this time to catch up on progress we were making in development and discuss any challengers or decisions that had to be made to keep things moving along. This was also the forum for me to spring new screwy ideas I had dreamed up—I'd roll out my thoughts, and he would patiently explain what laws of physics I was proposing to violate. As you may have gathered, I am not the most detailed person in the world, and I tend not to let reality interfere with a cool idea until faced with incontrovertible proof that it won't work (in this universe, anyway).

Most days I could ramble on about things, and he would let me talk while he continued working on some prototype or whatever, but there was one phrase that caught his attention and would cause him to stop what he was doing and give me his full attention. The five most terrifying words he ever heard were, "You know, I've been thinking." He knew when he heard this phrase (or something very similar) that I had an idea for a new product category and that if he didn't talk me out of it immediately, he would discover in a couple of days that I had coopted resources that should be used for something else to explore some crazy scheme. Most of the time, he could talk me off the ledge in a few minutes, and the danger would pass; but every once in a while, I would come up with something that was not only actually possible but also intriguing to him. We'd spend some time talking it through, and if it actually sounded promising, his comment would be, "Must be time to fire up the blender," which we both knew meant that he would be working late nights fueled by fruity rum drinks. I knew I could leave it at that as he would think about it for a while and work through a plan to turn a load of BS into something useful.

I bring this up now partly to restate my belief that you need to surround yourself with people who not only have complementary skills to yours but also have complementary personalities. If you are the big-picture visionary type, do not go out and find people like yourself but rather find people whose personalities will drive you crazy—you need that balance. Picking the right cofounders is the most important decision you will make, so choose wisely.

The other reason I bring this up is to provide some insight as to how you can motivate engineers and other technical people. Like any other discipline, you will find a wide variety of personality types, and any motivational techniques will need to be tweaked for different individuals, but one thing is universal: the best technical people like nothing more than a challenge that others haven't achieved. Note that I said the "best" technical people—you can find engineers all day long who are happy to show up for work and do what they're told but just like any other personnel you hire; you don't want them. Let your competitors hire them and go for the ones who are looking to do something special. Period.

So far I have used the term engineer to describe any technical person you may employ, and in the old days that would have been literally true—anybody you hired for a technical job would have some sort of an engineering degree. In today's world, however, you may find that many of your key development personnel not only don't have a degree but may have never set foot in an engineering classroom, and it is important to understand the different personality types you may encounter. Before we get into the details of how to work with technical folks, let's provide some general classifications of people (though as

JIM LEWIS

with many jobs, these categories are not fixed boundaries, and hopefully you will find people who can wear multiple hats):

- Hardware engineers: These folks absolutely should be degreed and licensed professionals. Why? Simply put, you can screw up software and customers get angry; you screw up hardware, and customers get killed. Maybe I'm oversensitive about this, but for many years I designed and built products that connected to upward of six hundred volts, and I have zero incidents in nearly twenty-five years. It's one thing to stay up nights worrying about cash flow, but I don't even want to think about how much sleep I would lose if one of my products killed or severely injured someone. There is a place for what I call hobbyists (people who have built a lot of their own products and are likely to have a great deal of hardware knowledge) in your company, but hardware design is not one of them. Put them in tech support or engineering support and testing, but make sure somebody with a stamp is doing your design.

- Software engineers: This is a somewhat less defined category. Many engineers getting electrical engineering degrees today not only have experience in software but may actually have concentrated in software work. People who have degrees in engineering and have a blend of software and hardware are worth their weight in gold in a small company—they can focus most of their time in one realm or the other but also provide valuable backup for multiple areas and serve as checks and balances for other engineers on your team.

- Software developers: Use whatever term you want to describe these folks, but they all share one common characteristic: they do not have degrees (or they may have them in something like philosophy). They are into writing code because they love it, and for the most part, they've been at it for a good many years. They tend to be mercurial and work really weird hours, but never reject anyone out of hand who loves what they do and would happily do what you're paying them to do for free. They will work themselves to the point of exhaustion and bring with them a view of the world that is not colored by traditional engineering classes. This can be hugely valuable in a small company (and hated in big companies). If you have someone you trust to check their work, they can be very useful in specific applications—and if you or someone on your staff isn't competent to supervise, make sure you have really good lawyers. Also, don't put mandatory drug testing in your employee manual till you absolutely have to—not sayin', just sayin'.

- Contractors: These are engineers or companies of engineers who will take on specific projects for a fee, and they may be a decent option for ancillary projects that are a distraction to your direct employees. Many small companies are using Eastern European firms to do software development and find that they can get high-quality work at a very good price. In my view, they should not work on the core of your products, and you should have a very good attorney review any documents, but they could be useful for some things. For example, if you are building a product for industrial control that needs some user interface software, you might consider farming it out to an outside firm that specializes in user interface work, as much of what they have done will be readily adaptable to your products. A few cautions: (1) you have to support whatever they make, so be sure it's good; (2) make sure that you have a clearly defined end result and understand the terms; (3) if you outsource internationally, be prepared to accept the challenges of language and time difference in your working relationship; and (4) have every legal document review by counsel—nothing is worse than coming up with some really cool, unique interface and then seeing it used by the contractor's next customer on your dime.

With the exception of contractors, any of these employees will have an impact on your company culture, and you have to be ready for it. In addition to having a break room stocked with pork rinds and

Rockstar, you will likely find that the work habits of these people will be somewhat different than you are used to. Unlike Rick, these guys show up around eleven because they worked till 3:00 a.m. or later (this is especially true for software geeks, who tend to get on a roll and work till an issue is resolved). Other employees may resent the fact that the software team shows up when they feel like it and you have to be the one to mitigate the impact this will have on the rest of your team. Left to fester, these are the kinds of things that will cause major issues in the company, and you won't know it till a key player tells you he or she is leaving; so figure out in advance how you plan to address this.

Engineers and non-engineers (even though both are product development folks) probably have more differences than similarities, so we'll spend some time talking about their characteristics and how the nontechnical types can work with technical people effectively. Of course, we are painting with very broad strokes here, and (like with any population) there are many different traits to people with similar backgrounds, so take it all with a grain of salt.

Engineers are some of the most anal retentive people in the world, and this is a wonderful thing for society in general. They tend to see the world in black and white, yes or no, right or wrong, and so on. Why do I say this is a good thing? Well, imagine that the guy who designed the bridge you are on or built the sewer system that gets waste out of your house was the sort of person who approached the job with a "gee, I hope that works" attitude. Not good for bridges—and not good for your products, either. Even if you are not talking about potentially dangerous products (like meters connected to 480V), you don't want to be a year into shipping your first product all around the country (or world) and discover that the electrical design of part of the circuit pushed every component to the very limit of its capability. It all checked out fine at the factory, but after months of constant stress in the field, components begin to fail and you begin seeing products come back. This is not only extremely expensive but also creates a bad reputation for your company in the field. What do you suppose the odds are that a customer who has installed a dozen or so of your products and has had to go back to each of the buyers and replace the product is going to come back or refer your company to someone else? Not happening.

This is probably a great time to talk about product quality, as nothing is more important to your company than having things work right. Most people grossly underestimate the cost of poor quality (either in design or manufacture) and think that as long as you provide a decent warranty, your customers will be OK; but let's take a look at an example to see the real cost of poor quality. My first company started with a product that used electrical current draw by an electrical device like a fan to determine if the fan was working properly (not that anyone is all that interested, but if a belt breaks on a fan and the motor keeps running but no air is moving, the electrical current draw drops—aren't you glad you asked?). Anyway these sensors cost about twenty-five dollars to build and sold for about fifty dollars, so replacing a failed product would cost about twenty-five dollars plus the cost of shipping, right? From the company's perspective, yes, but let's assume the product is installed fifty miles from the contractor's office. Here's the contractor's cost to replace the unit:

Cost of replacement unit	$0
Trip to installation to troubleshoot	
Labor for drive and analysis	$150
Paperwork and return of unit	$50
Receipt of replacement and paperwork	$50
Return trip to install	$150
Gas, meals, and vehicle wear and tear	$75
Loss of profit on billable hours	$400
Total direct and opportunity cost	$875
Cost of a customer whose system is down for a week	Priceless

If you wonder why your customer wasn't thrilled that you replaced the unit for free, this should provide your answer. Now just imagine that your customer is in South Africa or that the installation is two hundred miles away, and replacing your fifty-dollar sensor ends up costing thousands of dollars. Hopefully I've made my point about why quality is critical and why you want engineers who won't let you build crap, no matter how hard you try.

So I'm saying that product failures are a total disaster, right? In the near term, yes—you have to drop what you're doing and scramble to replace a product with no compensation; your customer has to spend a small fortune and waste a day or two; and oh, by the way, the end user has a system that's down, and he or she is getting no benefit. It may be tough right now, but there actually is a silver lining if you look hard enough. Products fail, and no matter how hard you try, some of the things you make are going to die in the field. Everybody knows that. The most important thing you can do now is not make the situation worse by making your customer jump through hoops to get the product replaced. Over the long haul (assuming that your products don't develop a habit of blowing up), the customer will remember how you handled the problem—were you responsive, and did you and your team do everything to mitigate the damage? Not far down the road, the customer will remember how you dealt with the problem more than the problem itself, I promise.

So what can you do to turn this pile of lemons into lemonade? Let me share a practice that I started from day one at my first company and carried through till the day I sold the second one. If we couldn't troubleshoot a problem when the customer called in, my sales reps and tech support personnel were authorized to ship an advance replacement overnight. An advance replacement is just what it sounds like—we send out a new unit overnight so the customer has it in his hand when he goes to the jobsite. If the product is defective, he sends it back. As far as I know, this was unique practice (at least in our industry), and think about what it does—it saves the customer one trip at several hundred dollars, and, more importantly, it gets his or her client back up and running in a day instead of a week or more. Competitive advantage—what do you think? First of all, you are telling your customer that you are going to do everything possible to fix the problem; and second, if you go to all this trouble and expense, you clearly don't plan to do this very often (reinforcing your message of building quality products).

Over the years I've heard every imaginable objection to this policy, so let me see if I can anticipate some of the questions you probably have:

1. What if they don't send the failed unit back? This question is usually asked by the accountants, and the short answer is that we sent out an invoice with the unit that stated that if they didn't return the bad one within thirty days, they would pay for the replacement at market price.
2. How many failures did you have? Our average defect rate was less than 0.05 percent, so it wasn't high (and by the way, this policy gives you a great incentive to make sure your products are good, as replacement is very expensive and disruptive).
3. What if the product wasn't defective? Over the years I would guess that more than 80 percent of the advanced replacements we sent out turned out to be wiring or installation problems. So this must be a stupid idea, right? We spent a lot of time and money busting our butts to fix a problem that wasn't even ours in almost every case. Wrong, wrong, wrong! Put yourself in my customer's shoes: he called us to complain that we sold him junk, we moved mountains to get him a new unit, and it turned out to be his fault all along. Guess who's holding a big IOU? That's right—me.

In some cases we even discovered that we had a systemic problem with a newly released product—despite all our best efforts, something was either designed or installed incorrectly, our testing failed to catch it before it went out, and we had to do a product recall of multiple products from multiple customers. Ouch! When we had issues like this (and they weren't very frequent, thankfully), we would usually go to the customers preemptively with an offer not only to replace the product but to provide some additional compensation for the labor and hassle. If you ever do this, make sure that what you give away is not cash but product credit. Why? First, the money can only be spent with you; and second, one hundred dollars in product credit actually costs you only fifty dollars if you have a 50 percent gross margin.

Regardless of what product you are making, I hope you get the message: design it right, build it right, and support the hell out of it. Before we finish with product recalls and quality, I'll share one experience that proves the road to hell is paved with good intentions. At one point in my first company, we were suffering from some growing pains, and we had three products we had to recall in an eighteen-month period—ugh! To make things worse, if you're a sales rep with a cool new product, who is the first customer you call? Your best customer, of course; so we had our best customers who had suffered three recalls in a short period of time. The holidays were approaching, and our VP of Sales had a great idea. As we were based in the Pacific Northwest, we could send all of these customers a smoked salmon from Oregon for the holiday festivities. I thought it was a great idea, and we bought a case of salmon and sent it off. The response was outstanding as we had customers calling for days telling us how much they were looking forward to sharing the salmon with their families over Christmas. I think it was around December 23 when we started getting calls from these folks—turns out the salmon had been packaged improperly, and when they opened the foil, it released a stench that they had not been able to get out of the house for two days. Oddly enough, most of them had a sense of humor about it. I don't remember how we made it up to them, but I'm sure it was expensive.

It all starts with the best engineers, so how do you find them? As with any other hire, your best bet is somebody you know—maybe an engineer at the big company you worked for who was really sharp but hated the job. If not, your next best option is somebody who knows somebody or somebody who knows somebody who knows somebody who…never mind; you get it. I will expose my conservative roots by saying that most people who are looking for work are looking for work for a reason, and I know that there are exceptions, but in my experience really good people always have (or can easily find) work. This isn't always true, of course and I have little doubt that there are well-qualified people out there who are victims of circumstance, but in some cases, Darwin was right, and there you are. Same goes for people with a ton of companies on their résumés—if they were really good, somebody would have kept them.

One of the biggest things to avoid is someone who has spent his or her entire career working for a giant chip manufacturer. Odds are that the job consisted of following specific instructions about how to build a three-nanometer-square portion of a microprocessor that is the size of your fingernail. Unless you are well along and have a large engineering staff, you are going to be asking people to take ownership of a whole project, and this is such a different beast than such people are used to. You could actually see the person's brain explode before your eyes (just kidding, what will actually happen is that this engineer will push every decision, no matter how small, up to you or someone else). Big waste of his or her time—and yours. The only exception is if you happen to find the rare gem who does what he or she does to pay the bills but spends countless hours of his or her own time building some really cool stuff that the world has never seen. If you have that, then it's a maybe.

Assuming you can get engineers to come in and talk to you about a job, how do you get them to come aboard? The first thing they will ask about is money, not because engineers are greedy but because salary is an objective measure of value—and there is nothing engineers love more than objective measures. You can't pay them what they want or what somebody else will or what they're worth, so how do you get around this deal-killer? First, remember what I said before: the really good ones are looking for a challenge, the chance to do something no one else has done. They won't tell you that, because ego is subjective and they don't like subjective things, but in reality it's very important to them. They will tell you that they just want to build cool products that will garner peer recognition and envy, but tell them that this is a product that will be sold worldwide to thousands or millions of customers, and you will probably see an intrigued look. After all, how many engineers at a big company get the chance to be solely responsible for designing a product that millions of people use? Throw in some potential bonuses and the growth opportunities, and you just might set the hook.

Here's another tip: even if you don't volunteer the information that you are not an engineer, they will figure it out very quickly, and your status will plummet more quickly than you can imagine. Engineers respect other engineers, and anyone who is not an engineer is not very high on the food chain. You will never overcome this unless you get a degree yourself and prove your worth in the engineering world, and you don't have time for that; but there is something you can do: spend your personal time learning as much as you can about hardware and software and make some effort to put your ideas to work (seriously, I'm not kidding here). You can earn some props from real engineers by spending time writing code, even if it sucks. They always feel underappreciated, and if you show that you are putting some effort into it, they really respect it; and besides, it won't hurt you one bit to learn something about what your engineers are doing (remember, you're not an accountant, but you took a lot of accounting classes to get your degree). And it's actually pretty cool to make something happen on your computer besides winning at Solitaire. Many years ago, I wrote some code in C++ for a trade show we had coming up. I wanted to provide a graphic display of energy measurements from our meters, and I had bought some blenders and connected the meters to the blenders. The software would communicate via RS485 serial comms and produce a graphic display of the energy. I actually got it to work. I had absolutely pushed my programming skills to the limit and beyond as it required some fairly low-level manipulation of bits on the serial port (yes, I'm bragging a little, and it really was pretty cool). I had a really great software engineer, and I couldn't wait to show him what I'd done. I asked him to stop by my desk, and when he did I fired up this program. It worked like a charm, producing a graph that showed the change in energy with multiple blenders, and he was really impressed.

"That is really cool. You wrote that yourself?"

"Yes, I did. Wrote it all in C++, including the low-level serial port stuff and the screen graphics."

"Very nice. Mind if I look at the source code?" For nontechies, source code is the actual code running on the machine that makes it work, which the user never sees, and the key thing you want from code is for it to be efficient, transportable, and reliable.

"Sure, here you go." I was pretty sure he thought I had simply pulled some program off the web, and I was excited to show him that I actually had done all the code myself.

As he scrolled through the code, I watched one of the greatest displays of body language I have ever seen. He started with his hand at his side, reading, and then his right hand moved to his chin. The more he read, the higher his hand got on his face till it covered his mouth (for those not versed in body language, this meant he was physically trying to restrain himself from speaking). I could tell that he really wanted to tear into my programming, but he managed to restrain himself and instead came up with a simple question: "And this works?"

Of course I was crushed, but then he went on to explain that my code was poorly documented and that my approach was not the least bit elegant; it was really what he called brute force programming—it worked, but it was ugly.

The moral of this story isn't that I suck at programming (I do) but rather that at the end of his ripping my program to shreds, his closing comment was, "It's not great code, but I don't know how many company presidents would even take the time to try this, much less make it work. That's pretty cool." The thing is, you may never gain respect for your technical knowledge or skills, but your tech folks will respect the fact that you put in the time and effort, and that's worth its weight in gold. And this is true for every job in your company—you don't have to do it better than anybody else, but let them know that what they are doing is important to you, because if somebody is doing a job that isn't important to you, he or she needs to go.

Full disclosure time again. I've hired more than my share of nonengineers for technical jobs (tech support, production, etc.), but as I've primarily built hardware with some firmware inside and very little user interface software, I have limited experience with the classical software folks who work at Facebook and Google. What I do know about them is that they are different cats, but like most tech folks, their major motivation is the challenge and not the money. Figure out how to challenge them, and they will make really cool stuff—and they all know each other, so if you can find one, he or she can tell you where to find the others.

I have had some experience with contractors, and I'm not a big fan. It's hard to know exactly how much time they are spending on your project, and it is very difficult to make sure that you are on the same page with regard to quality and features. It can be challenging to keep the contractor focused, and even with specifications and timelines, the potential for miscommunication is very high. Add in using some Eastern European contractors, and you raise the complications to a whole new level. I know people who have done it with success, but it seems to me like a tough place to try and save a few bucks. Personally, I like to be able to walk down the hall and talk to the guy who wrote the code, understands how it works, and knows how to make changes and enhancements down the road.

I've talked a little bit about the ego balancing act that entrepreneurs face. You need a big enough ego to tackle challenges that others see as insurmountable but not so big that you are unable to look at things objectively and know where you are. The same can absolutely be said for engineers—they need to be willing to break new ground and accomplish things that most engineers wouldn't try but still remain unbiased about the progress they are making.

I learned this the hard way as I suffered through two disasters with different engineers that cost my company thousands of dollars—along with lost time and customers. In each case, I had very bright engineers who were tackling new product designs with untested approaches— the classic high-risk, high-reward scenario that start-ups thrive on—but things got out of control. After a few months of initial design and prototype building, each of the projects was ready to move into the crucial testing and validation stage, where breakthrough ideas can be proven (or disproven); lots of really cool products are killed off at this point. As with any mistake, the key is to admit it as soon as possible and take steps to mitigate the damage going forward. If something isn't working, that's a shame, but it's critical to kill off failures and move on to other projects. Unfortunately, both of these engineers had so much time and ego invested in their ideas that they were unable to face the reality that the test results were just not what they expected. At this point you would hope that they would be honest about the results and lay their cards on the table, so that decisions could be made, but egos overrode objectivity, and they chose to falsify or tweak test results to be much more encouraging than they really were. Weeks later when the real state of affairs became obvious, I confronted each of them in what I can honestly say were two of the most unpleasant meetings I have had in all my years. At first, each engineer denied doing anything wrong, but after being confronted with proof of what they had done, they reluctantly confessed to it. After listening to their explanations, it became clear that in each case, they felt that, although they weren't being completely honest, the only reason they had fudged the numbers because they were sure they could fix the problems and were afraid that the product would be killed before they had the chance to make it right.

This kind of issue is unlikely to occur at a large company where most people work in teams, have more technical supervision, and have dedicated product testing protocols, but in a small company the primary engineer is frequently the only engineer and, in most cases, does all of the design and testing alone. As the boss, you are constantly trying to balance the need to get cool products to market quickly but still have adequate testing to make sure that the quality and performance of the product is up to your standards. Hence, you will find yourself relying on people to be honest about where they are. Much as I would like to put all the blame on these two people, the reality is that as much (or more) of the blame lies with me as I had created a culture that put too much emphasis on breakthrough products and not enough on doing the right things. I learned some valuable (and expensive) lessons from these episodes:

- Build your technical knowledge: I've said it before, but it bears repeating that you need to spend time learning about the technical aspects of your products. Having knowledge of how the hardware and software work will allow you to ask questions that might uncover issues sooner.
- Hire people you can trust: This is where it's great if you can hire someone you know and trust. Hiring an engineer you don't know and failing to communicate priorities can be disastrous.
- Learn to read body language: Most people who are lying will do one of two things—they will either gloss over seemingly important topics or spend an inordinate amount of time explaining something that seems trivial. If you're not comfortable with explanations you are getting, ask more questions.
- Make your expectations and priorities clear: With reward comes risk, and it is critical that you make it clear that you expect there to be setbacks in the high-risk environment of your company. Many people come from environments where failure is punished, and it's up to you to overcome that.

One final note about the technical team you assemble: make sure that you make provision for tech support from the moment you ship your first product. This will fall to the design engineer initially, as you can't afford to hire tech support personnel. I can pretty much guarantee that your engineers will bitch and moan about having to provide tech support in addition to design, and they have a point. Engineers in design mode want to work with a minimum of distractions, and the unpredictable nature of customer calls makes this difficult. So there is no doubt that this has an impact on development, but that's just too bad. First, you don't have the cash to hire somebody, and that alone makes it an easy decision—but having engineers do tech support has an added benefit that might not be immediately obvious. Your engineers are designing products to meet customers' needs, but they rarely have contact with those customers to see what issues they are having; and taking tech support calls can be a real eye opener. Many times I've had engineers approach me with comments like, "You know, I've talked to quite a few installers, and it seems like most of their problems are in network setup. Turns out they almost always use DHCP instead of static IPs, so I was thinking maybe we should make DHCP the default and save them a step." Great educational exercise for them.

I also require the design engineers to write the assembly manual for production and to do the training of the production staff in how to build the products. This helps them understand the challenges production employees face in building products and will hopefully help them incorporate features to make assembly easier in future products. Too many times I have seen departments working in silos where the engineer's sole task is to design something that works, without regard to whether it is buildable. A lot of this may seem trivial, but it all adds to having engineers who "own" their products from cradle to grave and understand the customers' needs.

Now, you might think that Dave Lavin, being an engineer himself, would have little trouble finding and managing engineers; and as you may recall, he needed a good hardware engineer to take his prototype design and make it functional and buildable. He'd stayed in touch with many of his classmates and was hoping to find someone there who fit what he needed, but he found that everyone he talked to either had just started another job or had too little practical experience to do what he needed. After tapping into every network he could think of, Dave meets with one of his professors to see if he knows anybody who might be available. Dr. Schulman is a guy Dave likes, and his specialty is more on the hardware side, so Dave is hopeful he could help. He goes to Dr. Schulman's office to meet with him.

"Dr. Schulman, thanks for taking the time to talk with me. Based on what I told you on the phone, do you think you can help?"

"Before we talk specifics, I just want you to know you that I think it's great you are doing this," Dr. Schulman told him. "I really enjoy seeing my students getting out there and taking chances, and I've been thinking about this since you called. You mentioned that you've contacted the people from class that you thought might be possible without much success, right?"

"Not much success is being kind, believe me. I thought that since I had a basic working design, finding somebody to finish it off would be pretty easy, but this is driving me nuts and eating up a huge amount of time that I don't have right now."

"I know it may seem to you like it's just 'finishing it off,' but as you may recall, I spent a lot of time talking about the differences between building a prototype with no real estate or cost constraints and fitting that some product into a design package with a cost target."

"Yeah, you're right, but still…"

"But nothing. I took a quick look at the parts list you sent over, and even using all surface-mount parts in the smallest packaging and a micro with integrated memory, you're still looking at a four-layer board at least—probably a six-layer, given the size of the package you want to fit it in. That type of design needs somebody who isn't doing his first rodeo."

"Well, I was thinking about an ASIC."

"Were you paying any attention at all in my class, or did you just hack into the server and change your grade to pass? To do an ASIC, you need to have a rock-solid feature set that won't change for years, eighteen months for development, and deep, deep pockets. Not to mention a market that will allow you to build in huge volumes—none of which you have, correct?"

"True."

"OK, so we're back to finding somebody who can do a multilayer board on a modest budget in a few months."

"Yep. Would you be interested?"

"The project sounds interesting, but my plate is already full; and besides, there are major issues with the university regarding any intellectual property I create. Believe me, you don't want the Board of Trustees here as partners."

"So you're saying I'm screwed."

"Well, as I said, I've been thinking about this quite a bit and there is one option that comes to mind."

"Sweet! Sign me up."

"Hold your horses, there are some challenges."

"Like what?"

"The guy I'm thinking of is Dick Cochran. He came through here a few years ago, and I can honestly say that he is one of the brightest guys I ever taught. The first issue is that you wanted to hire somebody as an employee, and Dick is working as an independent contractor. Since you have your EE and understand the hardware, it's maybe not as big an issue."

"I can live with that. And maybe it's an advantage since there's no conflict, and he could start pretty soon. You said 'challenges' with an *s*, so what else is there?"

"Well, I haven't spent a lot of time with Dick lately, but I do recall that he had some, uh, quirks."

"Quirks? Like what?"

"You know, I don't want to prejudice your discussion, and I really think he could knock this out for you easily, so why don't you just give him a call? You can tell him I referred you, and I imagine he'll at least listen."

"Quirks, huh?"

"Yeah, quirks. But most engineers have some, so don't let it worry you."

Driving away from the school, Dave isn't sure how he feels. On the one hand, for the first time in weeks, he has a solid lead on somebody to do the work, but he could swear that he heard a chuckle in Schulman's voice whenever he mentioned quirks. Given his limited options, Dave calls Cochran, and they guy sounds not only normal but also genuinely excited about the project, and they schedule an interview for the next day. The next day after discussing Dick's background (which sounds great), Dave is feeling good about the possibilities. Dick has even raised the option of working on some sort of commission or license basis in lieu of some or all of the hourly fees for consulting, which Dave hadn't thought of.

"Dick, I'm not going to bullshit you, I like everything I hear, and I think you might be a good fit for us."

"I'm glad you think so, Dave. I'm excited by the opportunity and the challenge this thing presents, and I hope we can work something out."

"Cool, let's talk about schedules. How soon can you start?"

"Got a couple of things I'm cleaning up, but that should take about a week, so I can be good to go a week from Monday."

"Great, it would probably be best if you worked from here, so if you have any questions, I'd be right here."

"You have Internet, right?"

"Of course. It's just DSL, but we do get pretty good upload and download speeds, so you shouldn't have any—"

"I don't think you understand. I can't work on any computers or systems that are connected to the web at all."

"Oh, I see, so…wait, what?"

"I never use a computer or phone connected to the Internet—and neither should you."

"I'm confused."

"Look, kid, it's really very simple. You know how much value governments (ours and theirs) put on top engineers, right?"

"Um, OK."

"A few years back, I started noticing some strange things happening when I was on a computer connected to the Internet—weird sounds coming from the speakers, flickers on the screen—you know."

"OK."

"OK, so I wrote some code to catch the analog signals being sent to the screen and the speakers (and the printer, too) and found some very interesting things. You're familiar with phi, right?"

"You mean the golden ratio? One point six one eight, going on forever but never repeating."

"Top marks, son. Now looking at the analog signals on a scope and matching signal frequencies I discovered that the frequencies of the first, sixth and eighteenth time blocks corresponded to the letters *n*, *s*, and *a*. Get it? One, six, eighteen? One point six one eight, and that's no coincidence."

"Meaning…?"

"Jesus, can I be any clearer? NSA! The damn government was monitoring what I was doing and where I was so the Pentagon could grab me and put me in one of their secret facilities to work for them, so I stopped using anything where they could track me."

"Sounds a little unusual, but if you work from home, how do we get the design work as you finish it?"

"Hand to hand, only way."

"So you'll bring it over once a week or so."

"No way; it takes me almost three hours to get here with the lousy bus connections."

"Can't you just drive them over?"

"Have you heard anything I said? Cars have satellite radio, GPS, and all kinds of tracking systems, so there's no way in hell I'm getting in one of those."

"So we'll send somebody over to your place to pick up the files, and…"

"Negatory, son. As soon as they track you folks coming over to my place and tap into your computers, they'll know what I'm up to, and I'm a dead man. We'll meet at different locations from a code chart I'll give you and keep it random. And be sure to send somebody who's not an engineer to avoid suspicion."

"I'll have to get back to you, Dick. Is it OK if I call?"

"Sure, it's a landline, and I have better stuff than the White House for encryption."

Needless to say, Dave never called and instead ended up hiring another contract firm to complete the hardware design.

10

ACCOUNTING AND FINANCE

I'm sure many of you have been asking yourselves, "When are we going to talk about accounting some more?" Well, your prayers are answered as we are going to dedicate an entire chapter to this topic (technically, topics as accounting and finance are related but some-what separate).

OK, let's be honest: even accountants think accounting is bor-ing. But boring or not, you really need to have an understanding of accounting. If you don't have a business background, you absolutely have to take a course in both financial accounting and managerial accounting. Why do I regard accounting as such a critical part of your business? Let me provide you with some reasons.

1. **You can't manage what you can't measure.** This phrase is fre-quently used in many different business contexts, but nowhere is it more important than money. You need the most accurate, timely information you can get your hands on.
2. **Trust, but verify.** Have you ever picked up your local paper and read where a bookkeeper for a local plumbing company (or scout troop or whatever) embezzled $100,000 from the com-pany over three years? Yes, the bookkeeper is to blame and should be punished, but in my view the owner of the company bears a great deal of responsibility. If someone steals one hun-dred grand from your small business and you don't know it, you are not running your company, end of story.

3. **No surprises.** I never cease to be amazed at the number of small business owners who have no idea how their companies have performed financially until they turn the financials over to the tax accountant at the end of the year. The IRS has zero tolerance, and if you suddenly discover that you owe fifty grand in taxes that you didn't plan for, you are royally screwed.

4. **Report card.** If you are using your accounting and financial reports only for cash flow and tax purposes, you are missing out. Timely financial information can let you know about operational problems—for example, a drop in gross margin is not just an accounting issue; it likely also shows that something is wrong in your operations. Maybe your build cost went up, maybe your sales reps are selling at cheap prices, or whatever, but it is information you absolutely need to know.

This is not the appropriate forum for a fundamentals-of-accounting primer, but I will provide some basic concepts about accounting and financials primarily for the purpose of demonstrating what is different about a small company's financials and some key things to look out for.

Although there are a lot of important concepts and reports that have meaning for investors, large companies, and tax authorities, there are really only two reports that are critical to the small business owner: the income statement and the balance sheet. When you hear people talk about seeing the financials, it is these two reports they are usually referring to, and they are also the most important to you in building and running your new venture. They have very different uses, so it's important to know what info each can provide about your business (and as the company grows, the importance of each will change).

Before we look into some of the details of reports from accounting, let me remind you once again that you absolutely need to spend the time and money to set up your accounting system long before you start selling products. You need to record and categorize your start-up expenses, and this will be far easier if you have a system that will let you assign your costs to specific cost centers. Far more important, if you have a system in place with revenue accounts and standard costs, when your sales rep enters that very first order, all he or she has to do is enter the customer information and select the product purchased and quantity, and the software does the rest. It automatically adds the total sales (sell price times quantity) to the revenue account and also adds the COGS (standard cost times quantity) to the monthly COGS account, generates an invoice, and creates a receivable. Another bid advantage is that having a software program lets you plug in the standard price of a product that appears automatically and doesn't let reps charge whatever they want. Go online, get a copy of QuickBooks, and have your accountant spend a few hours setting it up—and do it now.

Income Statement

The income statement is the single most important report you can have, so pay attention. Basically, the income statement is a snapshot of the company's performance for a specific period of time (day, week, month, quarter, year, etc.). It tells you how much revenue you brought in for that time, what the direct cost of the products sold was, how much you spent on overhead, and the all-important bottom line number for net income. Let's take a look at each of these pieces:

- **Revenue**—this is a measure of the value of products you shipped during the period (critical note: this is very different than how much cash you brought in). It is the sum of all the invoices you sent out during the period, which is pretty easy to get. This may be very different from what was sold as you may very well have received orders for products that have not shipped (this is the difference between booked revenue and billed revenue, and not knowing the difference has landed some people in jail).
- **Cost of goods sold (COGS)**—this is pretty simple. It is a measure of what it cost you to build the products that you

shipped and invoiced for and is matched to the revenue you generated. This is not a measure of how much raw materials you bought or actual labor that you paid for in the month but rather the cost of materials and labor contained in the products you shipped—big difference and big impact on cash flow. Your accountant will establish what is known as a *standard cost* for each product, and this is what is used for COGS.

- **Gross profit**—this is simply the mathematical difference between revenue and COGS (subtract COGS from revenue, and you have gross profit dollars).

- **Gross margin percentage**—the formula is simple: gross profit (GP) divided by revenue, usually expressed as a percentage of revenue. This provides a quick and dirty operational performance review and is one you will use often.

- **Operating expenses**—these are essentially your fixed costs. Things like engineering, sales, and administration are the most common categories. This number reflects what you actually spent during the period for all of these areas (rent, salaries, insurance, etc.).

- **Operating income**—this is basically GP minus operating expenses for the period.

- **Other income and expenses**—for some reason, accountants have to take some items and put them separately (interest expense, depreciation), so you just have to deal with it.

- **Net income**—not surprisingly, the net income number is operating income net of other income and expense. This is a big deal number for a lot of reasons (not the least of which is that this is the number that will be used to value your company when you sell).

Again, this is not intended to be a detailed analysis of accounting, so we will focus on a few of these measures that are most critical to running the business and talk about what you should be looking for.

Revenue

I don't want to belabor the point, but it is just as important to understand what revenue is not as to know what it is. It is not the total POs you got from customers or the amount of cash that you brought in this month; it is simply the total amount you billed customers for products that went out the door this month. In fact, if a customer prepays for an order for some reason (for example, a wire transfer in advance for an international order), it shows up on the books as a liability—no kidding, somebody gives you money and it's a liability. If this sounds like a small detail, it's not. For one thing, the friendly folks at the IRS will view revenue as the basis for determining your income and taxes, and they couldn't care less if the customer doesn't pay you—you still owe the taxes. The cash is your problem, not theirs, and this can be absolutely crucial in managing your business.

Determining revenue is a fairly straightforward process if you are shipping a product, as it is easy to know when the revenue should be recorded—it's when the product ships. As one example, imagination that you own a construction company that has bid a contract with a fixed price to be delivered over the course of two years. You obviously can't record the revenue up front, as you haven't delivered the completed job, but you certainly don't want to wait till the project is completed to send out a bill so what do you do? Most companies have some means of doing what is known as progress billing where the contractor is allowed to bill for some portion of the labor), but this creates the potential for questionable accounting. For instance, do you record revenue when materials purchased for the project arrive on site or when they are actually installed? And what is the COGS for an hour of labor if the worker was on overtime and can you bill more that hour than a regular hour? I'm sure you can see the potential for abuse or confusion when trying to determine how much revenue to realize and when to show it on your income statement.

COGS

In theory, cost of goods sold is a very simple concept—just add up whatever you spent to build a product, right? Consider a couple of complications. What if the production employee who builds Product A and is paid twelve dollars an hour goes on vacation and is replaced by another worker making thirteen dollars an hour? What is your labor cost for the month? Or what if in the first half of the month you were using parts purchased months ago, and in the second half you used parts you had to order on short notice at twice the price? What is the right cost for that part? Sure you can spend a lot of time and money tracking each product and its actual associated costs, but believe me, in most cases, the costs of tracking the costs will outweigh any benefits. Accountants get around this problem by creating standard costs for each product that reflect the average cost of labor and materials for the product. Of course, because you are using averages, the only thing you know for sure about the standard cost is that it is wrong, but it's the best you have; and if done with a reasonable amount of diligence they are pretty good. You may adjust standard costs if you have significant changes to the actual costs, but for the most part they are recalculated every six months or so to make them more accurate. You simply plug the standard cost into the accounting system, and each time a product is shipped, the COGS is calculated.

Gross Margin Percentage

I skipped gross profit because it is simply a calculated number and doesn't provide much useful information to the owner of the business. Gross margin percentage (GM%), on the other hand, is one of the most useful measures of the health of the company. A drop in GM% from one month to the next indicates a problem that needs attention—it could be caused by product mix, extraordinary costs, or discounts in pricing, but this is likely to be your first warning that something may be wrong and can allow you to fix issues quickly. The biggest use of GM% is a relative measure—that is, relative to last month, last year, or whatever. There are not a lot of objective measures of GM% as it is largely industry-dependent, but it is usually considered good for a manufacturing company to produce margins of 50 percent—more is better, of course, but this will give you some target to shoot for. This is another reason for having a good accounting system—you can get GM% not only for the whole company but also on a product by product basis, which can help you determine which products are really making money and where you need to invest your time and money to maximize profits.

Operating Expenses

These are costs that are recurring and fairly consistent, regardless of how much product you build or sell. This includes salaries for nonproduction personnel, rent utilities, and so on; and unlike COGS, these are the actual costs you incurred in these areas for the month or other period. These costs are generally grouped into three categories by department or function:

- Sales and marketing—costs associated with selling your products and include salaries, commissions, travel, and entertainment as well as advertising and other marketing expenses. Obviously, these costs will vary based on your sales channels, but a good target for sales expense is somewhere around 13 percent of revenue; and if this number varies greatly month to month, you need to find out why.
- Engineering—basically the cost of developing your products, which includes salaries, tooling, contract engineering, regulatory testing and approvals, and any other required processes to get a product ready for production. Again, there are different targets based on industry, but you should probably assume that you will need to spend around 11 percent of revenue to keep your products current and to stay competitive.
- Administration—these costs are all of the costs that are related to the company in general rather than specific departments.

This includes your salary (if you have one); accounting and finance personnel; and other items like rent, CAM charges, insurance, and utilities. This should be in the neighborhood of 6 percent of revenue for most small companies. As your company grows, some of these costs like rent and utilities will likely be divided up and assigned to individual departments (usually based on square footage each group occupies), and you may eventually break them down to assign overhead costs to individual products. This can be very useful in figuring out exactly how much profit each product brings in. For example, a product that occupies twice the floor space will carry twice the overhead allocation, and this makes it easy to know where you are making money.

- Net income—the reason you have an income statement is so that it can tell you how much income you have made in the month. Net income is critical because, ultimately, net income turns into the cash you will use to fund operations, buy parts, and pay taxes. And oh, by the way, if your company makes $10,000 this month, and you own 70 percent of the company, you made $7,000 this month. Does that mean you can write yourself a check for seven large? No because the $10,000 first has to go to finance receivables, inventory, capital equipment, and a whole bunch of other things before you get whatever is left—if there is any. Also remember that the value of your company is generally determined as a multiple of net income, so if you made $250,000 in net profit last year, it is probably worth something like $2.5 million (pretty cool, huh?)

For large, stable companies with relatively slow growth, the balance sheet is very important, largely because there are critical measures that investors look at (like return on assets) that are dependent on maintaining a strong balance sheet. A strong balance sheet can also influence behavior, as companies with large cash hoards are more likely to make acquisitions for growth rather than investing in their own operations. For small companies the balance sheet has some use, but the income statement is far more important for running the business, maintaining the cash flow to stay solvent and tracking variances in critical measures.

Balance Sheet

The income statement is a measure of performance for a specified period whereas the balance sheet is essentially a report as of a particular date on the cumulative performance since the company's inception. I'm sure any accountants reading this just cringed at that description, but it's how I think of it; it's my book, and if you don't like it, you can write your own. The balance sheet has just three components: assets, liabilities, and owners' equity. Assets are just what you would expect: cash, money owed to you, and property you own. Liabilities are primarily things like accounts payable, debt, and other obligations. Owners' equity is what's left over after you subtract liabilities from assets. How many of the actual numbers are derived is a bit complicated, involving things like depreciation and amortization, but there are some pieces of the balance sheet are useful, particularly looking for relative changes over some period. Some of the key elements for small business owners to look at and keep an eye on are described below.

Assets

- **Cash.** No explanation required, I hope. You may have read that companies like Apple and Microsoft are fighting with investors because they have too much cash on their balance sheets (in Apple's case, $100 billion plus). When you have this problem, your best strategy is…just kidding, you'll never have this problem.
- **Accounts receivable (A/R).** You may think this is just like cash, and it sort of is, but this can definitely be a wolf in sheep's clothing. This is money that your customers owe you for products they have bought—and assuming they pay you on time,

it's great—but there are some things to be aware of with A/R. Having a growing receivables number is a good thing as long as your receivables are growing at the same rate as your sales. Remember that you are essentially a banker, loaning money to your customers. If your A/R is growing faster than your sales, you may have customers who are either not paying their bills or are dragging out payments and might be in trouble. One of the best metrics for tracking A/R is called DSIR (Days Sales in Receivables), which is basically a measure of how many days of sales you have in receivables. This metric should remain fairly stable even if sales are growing. Once you determine that a debt is not collectible, you want to write it off as soon as possible—it's painful, of course, and reduces your company's net worth, but you want to do it sooner rather than later. It's tempting to carry it on the books as an asset, but you need to take the hit for a couple of reasons: first, having bad debt on your books will give you overstated expectations for the cash flow you need to survive; and second, the IRS doesn't care that you can't collect this money. Your tax bill is based on sales, not how much money you get. The only thing worse than not getting money you are owed is having to use cash to pay taxes on the money you are not collecting, adding insult to injury.

- **Other assets.** There are some other asset items like property, intellectual property, pre-paid expenses, and so on, but these kinds of assets are unimportant in many businesses, particularly in the daily operations and management of the company. Things like intellectual property may become important if you are looking to value the company for sale but in

Liabilities

- **Accounts payable (A/P).** A/P is the flip side of receivables and is money you owe to suppliers for parts and services you have purchased. There are a couple of differences between A/R and A/P: first, being a small company, you will have much less generous terms from your suppliers than your big customers beat out of you, so you need much more in receivables than in payables to stay afloat; and second, even though some of your A/R will never be collected, you will pay all of your A/P if you want to stay in business.

- **Short- and long-term debt.** Odds are, all of your debt is short-term, and you probably don't have much of that yet. It will take a while before you can convince a bank to loan you money (even with the dreaded personal guarantee), and the only time most small companies have long-term debt is if some form of investment is treated as a loan rather than a direct equity investment.
- **Other liabilities.** There are some other liabilities like prepaid sales, but they don't matter much to you at this point.

There are more balance sheet ratios than you can count, and accountants and investors are inventing new ones all the time, mostly to justify investments people have made in companies that have no income and need some way to explain their enthusiasm. The ratios you care about as a small business owner are the ones related to your ability to pay your bills and remain solvent. The first is the current ratio, which is basically the ratio between current assets and current liabilities (CA/CL), and you want the number to be as large as possible (most people will say that you want at least two to one to be in good shape). The problem with the current ratio, as you may have deduced, is that you may not collect all of your receivables; and there is a timing difference between when you will collect your money and when you will have to pay, so if you are looking at balance sheet ratios, I prefer the acid ratio. The acid ratio basically compares cash to current liabilities (Cash/CL) and is a much better indicator of liquidity as cash is real and predictable. Obviously the acid ratio will be lower than the current ratio, but just know that if you have anything close to one to one, you are in great shape and can stop looking at numbers and move on to something really important.

One reason I say that the income statement is more important to you than the balance sheet is that troubling information from the income statement (e.g., falling GM%) is usually actionable—you can take steps to find out why the GM% is falling and hopefully fix it. Balance sheet information (e.g., acid ratio) is what it is, and there isn't much you can do about it in the near term—other than some bad things like not paying your bills or not sending in the money you withheld from your employees for taxes or social security. If you have liabilities that you shouldn't have incurred, you can make sure that the mistakes aren't repeated, but you are unlikely to be able to get out of paying your debts.

Owners' Equity

Owners' equity (OE) sounds like some deeply calculated reflection of the value owners have in a company (and technically, it is), but keep in mind that it has very little practical value and is simply what is left over when you subtract liabilities from assets. This is one of those places where accountants create a very simple means of making the balance sheet balance. Because the immutable laws of accounting say that Assets = Liabilities + Owners' Equity, all you have to do is dump any excess (or losses) from this equation into OE. It may make you feel good to see OE going up, and it is a good thing, but remember that beyond feeling good and making your mom proud, it has no practical use—you can't cash part of it in without selling some of your equity; and banks aren't usually interested in making loans against anything that can't be readily converted to cash, so don't get too excited.

Building Your Accounting Department and Team

I've mentioned accounting software several times already, mainly because it is really important and fairly easy to set up when you are getting started and a major pain in the butt if you wait till you really have to have it. I've referenced QuickBooks, primarily because I used it in both of my companies; and from what I can tell, it is the de facto choice for most small companies—as I noted earlier, it worked well enough for me that I was able to grow companies to over $10 million in revenue using the software—with upgrades, of course. I'm sure there are other programs out there, and this is not an endorsement of QuickBooks. Regardless of what program you choose, you will find that there are a lot of options and cool things you can do with your accounting software. I have little doubt that much of this is useful, but you don't want to spend a bunch of time and money on features of the software that are not absolutely critical to getting your business off the ground. Some of the critical things you want your accountant to set up at the start include the following:

- Chart of accounts: this is the core of functionality of your accounting software, and it involves setting up accounts for all of your activities (revenue, purchases, salaries, bonuses, etc.) by department or product class. Once you have these accounts set up, the reports and accounting become fairly automatic. As an example, let's say that you have two product categories that you will be building (for instance, in my case we had data acquisition products and wireless communications products), and you want to set up different revenue and cost accounts for each one so that you can track total sales, margins, and profit not only for the whole company but for each product line individually, which will prove useful later. Once you have the revenue accounts established and assign a product to that account, each time a rep enters an order for that product, the revenue (and COGS) are automatically loaded into the accounts and appear on the income statement or balance sheet in the appropriate places.
- Finished goods part numbers: you want to make sure that you have part numbers assigned to each product (and each variation of each product) and have these part numbers associated with revenue and cost accounts for the reasons outline above.
- Finished goods pricing: this is the time to set up any pricing categories you can anticipate based on your go to market

strategy. You should have different price levels for the same product for different customer types (end users, distributors, VARs, original equipment manufacturers (OEMs), and so on), and it can be really helpful to keep a couple of things in mind about having fixed pricing for each customer type:

o Be consistent. The easiest way to be sure that you are consistent in your pricing is simply to have one base price for your primary customer type and make the others a multiple of that number. That way, you only have to plug in one price, and the rest are calculated for you when you add new products.

o Protect your channel. Let's say that your primary strategy is to sell to VARs, who in turn will mark it up and sell it to contractors who will mark it up and sell it to end users. There are two strategies for protecting your VARs: (1) refuse to sell to end users and contractors and (2) have pricing tiers for contractors and end users that reflect the same markup (or more), so there is no reason for end users and contractors to bypass your VARs. The biggest drawback to refusing to sell to end users or contractors is that you may change your strategy down the road and build products for end users, and you will have made them angry. Setting price tiers leaves you flexibility while protecting your channel.

o Margin control. Now, I'm not saying that sales reps left on their own will cut prices to get a sale...oh never mind, that's exactly what I'm saying, and this can quickly develop into a major problem for gross margins. One way to deal with this is to set up processes for tracking sales prices or having someone review every sale, but the easiest way to handle this is to set prices for customer types—and do not give reps the ability to change them without getting approval from upper management. This has a lot of advantages in addition to protecting your margins, the most important being that all customers of the same type will pay the same price (other than potentially some volume based discounts, which can also be set in your system). Employees change jobs within all industries, and customers will quickly learn if a competitor is getting better pricing and this will protect you.

- Standard costs: this is the time to come up with standard costs for each of your products. At best you are making a SWAG (scientific wild-ass guess), but you need to have something in there—you can always tweak it later. You need to tie the pricing to the part number and also assign it to a cost of sales account for that product.
- Operating expense accounts: these are the accounts where you assign bills and expenses as they come in. You can assign specific recurring expenses (e.g., rent) to specific expense accounts so that when the bookkeeper enters a rent bill, it is automatically assigned to that account and department (or departments).

I'm sure I've left some things out that you will need to have, and different types of companies have different needs and will need different structures, but what I've outlined here will be enough to get you going in most cases. The most important thing is to get it done, and the second most important is to design a structure that will allow you to grow without having to redo the initial structure that you designed. You should be able to rely on your accountant to help with the initial setup, and this is probably a good time to talk about staffing.

Staffing

Hiring people to handle things like finance, accounting, and other front office tasks can be very difficult for entrepreneurs. It's much easier to justify hiring a sales rep who will bring in revenue or an engineer who will give you a cool new product to sell than to hire someone who does not have a direct impact on building or selling products. It may seem like small consolation, but try to keep in mind that if you need to hire someone for this department, it's because you actually have a viable business with sales coming in and the need to purchase raw materials to replace the products you are selling.

The first thing you need is an accountant. At this stage this is not someone you employ but rather someone you hire on an hourly basis. The primary tasks for your accountant at this point include:

1. setting up your accounting system and software;
2. consulting with your office staff and bookkeepers as needed to answer questions;
3. monthly visits to the company to close the books (prepare the financial reports and clean up any issues);
4. quarterly reviews with management to examine any issues and develop short-term goals;
5. annual assistance in building the business plan for the next year; and
6. preparation of materials for delivery to the tax accountant prior to April 15.

It's important to know what you are looking for. You want someone who has a lot of experience with small companies (preferably those with a similar corporate structure like an LLC) and not just the lady who does your personal taxes. The closer you can get to someone who works with companies just like yours (similar size, industries, etc.), the better, as your accountant is not learning at your expense and knows not only how others have handled issues similar to those you confront but also what the priorities are. As with your attorney, you really want to hire someone you know if possible, but at the very least ask around and get referrals from people you know who run small companies. Unless you have someone you know and are absolutely sure of, try to line up face-to-face meetings with potential candidates to determine not only their knowledge and experience but also how well their personalities will fit. This is a key player on your management team who, like everybody else on the team, will need to be a good fit with everyone else. Good ones don't come cheap, but you get what you pay for, and you will likely find that hiring the low bidder will ultimately cost you more than getting someone good.

Be prepared for the fact that you will actually need two accountants (or accounting firms)—one to do the financial accounting and keep the books on an ongoing basis and another to handle your taxes. I know that the accountant you hire to do the books is a CPA and might be able to do your taxes, but this is a bad idea for a couple of reasons. First, tax law is a moving target, and you need someone who is specialized and stays current on tax laws and changes. Second, it is always a good idea to have someone independent look at your books no matter how much you trust your primary accountant. By the way, if, during your interviews, someone suggests that he or she can do both, you should be very suspicious, as this is a sign that this person is more concerned with billable hours than with taking care of your company.

Now that you have your accountant and your accounting system up and running, it's time to figure out how you are going to handle the day-to-day operation of the accounting department. Somebody needs to enter and print orders, generate invoices, create purchase orders, and pay bills; and you certainly don't want to pay the accountant one hundred dollars an hour for data entry, so you need another option. Actually, you have a few options:

- Do it yourself. It's not glamorous, and it hardly feels like CEO work, but on the other hand you can stay around the office for a couple of extra hours and save yourself hiring someone who is going to cost you three or four grand a month that you can use somewhere else and given the choice between investing time and investing money, time is cheap.
- Sweet-talk someone into doing it for you part time, cheap or for free. In my case, my wife was working part time at the bank and was able to put in a few hours a week to handle the basic bookkeeping till we got up and running. I'm pretty sure she still has a complaint with the Labor and Industries board at

the state of Oregon for back pay as I don't think she ever got paid for the time she spent at the first company. This is really nice because it lets you add hours as needed without hiring someone for a full-time job.

- Take a look at hiring someone who is willing to handle a wider range of jobs to turn multiple part-time jobs into a single full-time slot. You may find someone who is capable of doing a little assembly work, help out in engineering, and answer phones in addition to bookkeeping and data entry and allow him or her to evolve into a full-time office manager role as the company grows.
- Use a temp service. Temporary agencies can be a great source of employees for a number of roles that you have, and there are several advantages to doing it this way. Temp employees can work part time and add hours as needed, you get a chance to see how they work with you and other employees, the temp service pays their benefits and handles payroll, and you can usually hire them as full-time down the road with little or no cost. The only real downside to using temps is that the cost per hour is relatively high, and you may lose them to another employer after spending time on training.

However you decide to handle this, keep in mind that it will change dramatically as the company begins to grow and as with any other job you need to make sure that you hire someone who can deal with a somewhat malleable job description. This is a role like many others that will start off as a jack-of-all-trades positions, evolve to full time bookkeeping, and likely be divided up as the company grows.

Using Accounting and Finance to Manage Your Business

Even if you have experience in accounting, either through education or personal experience, you need to be aware of some of the differences in running a small company and managing a part of a larger firm. The most important adaptation you will have to make is realizing just how critical cash flow is to your business. If you manage a branch office or department for a large company and you have a bad month, the primary repercussions you face are a report with brackets around the bottom line and a nasty phone call or e-mail from your boss. Have the same bad month and lose money in your little company, and you may find that you don't have the cash to pay your bills or your employees—not a happy place to be. Even more challenging is that you can have a great month with high growth, strong sales, and net income and face even larger cash challenges. If you think that sounds crazy, you're not alone, but let me walk you through a real-world example to show you what I mean.

My last company had several straight years of over 100 percent annual growth. This is, of course, exactly what you want and is cause for celebration (T-shirts for everyone!), but it can put some major pressure on your cash supply. To understand why this happens, you need to break this growth down from an annual number to monthly numbers, where the month-to-month revenue growth is around 10 percent. This is really not the place for a detailed explanation of why this kind of growth eats cash, but let me give you a summary of the problems:

- Turning A/R into cash: Remember how we talked about your customers beating you up for terms? If you sell $100,000 in January, you won't see that cash till March, and your actual cash collections for January are only around $80,000 from sales you made in October. So even though you report the $100,000 as revenue, you only have $80,000 in real money.
- Buying inventory to meet the growth: To sustain the 10 percent monthly growth, you will need to buy raw materials this month to build enough products to ship $110,000 next month; so at 50 percent margin, it will cost you about $55,000 in real money as you do not have as much float on purchases and labor is paid in real time.
- Your friends at the IRS: Here's where the real pain comes. The IRS doesn't give a crap when you get your money, and if you

are running at 20 percent net income, you made $20,000 this month, and they want their share in estimated taxes. For our purposes, we'll say is 30 percent or $6,000. And all the staff you needed to support $100,000 in sales gets paid in real dollars, even though you only really collected $80,000 in real dollars.

So by the end of the month you will have collected $82,500 that you have available to spend. You need around $55,000 to pay for raw materials and labor to build the products to ship next month, so you have $27,000 left. From that you have to pay $30,000 in operating expenses (30 percent of $100,000), so you now have $3,000; and the IRS is standing at the front of the line to get the $6,000 you owe them for estimated taxes, so your actual cash position at the end of the month is roughly $9,000 in the hole. I'm sure many, if not most, of you don't believe me, so here's your homework assignment: fire up Excel and plug in six months of this growth with the assumptions I used above, and you'll find you're constantly chasing money. Drop the growth rate to 5 percent per month, and you are actually $2,000 ahead, which means that for you to pay yourself, you have to slow down your growth by 50 percent—welcome to the start-up world, baby!

Whether high growth is a disaster or not is largely dependent on what you want from the business—if you want to maximize the sale value of the company, high growth is a wonderful thing as you are working on an earnings multiple; so if the net income doubles every year, so does the value. If you make $250,000 this year, your company is worth $2.5 million; and if the net income doubles next year, it's worth $5 million; and if you own 70 percent...

If, on the other hand, you want to own the business for the long haul and maximize the amount of cash that flows to you as the owner from operations, growth that is too high is a killer, and you will work to limit it. Don't believe me? I had a friend who was hired to take over as president of a manufacturing company as the owner wanted to semi-retire and spend more time on his sailboat, funding his activities with cash from the company—a personal ATM. The owner was pretty sharp, and he understood this principle very well—so well, in fact, that my buddy had an incentive plan that peaked at 15 percent annual growth. Less than 15 percent, and the incentive was reduced; more than 15 percent, and it went down again—a classic bell curve. The owner had figured out that he needed some growth but not too much, and 15 percent maximized his return.

Another key difference you will encounter is how you handle things like depreciation. Because, as we saw above, the IRS doesn't care what you have for cash, you want to manage your business to reduce your tax burden. Many large companies like to stretch out depreciation to produce better net income results, but small companies that are profitable will take as much depreciation as soon as possible to avoid paying taxes on cash they don't have.

Just a few days short of the first anniversary of the company's founding, Dave Lavin finds himself driving to a 4:00 p.m. meeting with his accountant Mark at the Goosed Moose. Mark had called the day before and asked Dave to meet him at the Goose this evening—this wasn't all that unusual, as Mark and Dave had met there several times, usually to have a discussion about the lack of cash and who wasn't going to get paid. It was better to have these meetings outside the office, for obvious reasons, but Dave has no idea what Mark wants tonight as they had just met a few days earlier, and Mark had told him everything was good as far as cash flow was concerned. In fact, they were almost three months ahead of their plan, and the previous month had actually been a breakeven on the income statement (though not positive cash flow). After thinking it over, Dave is pretty sure he knows what Mark wants to talk about. Mark has been billing them $100 per hour instead of his usual $150, but that was in exchange for letting Mark fit them in around his schedule. Now they had been calling Mark a lot more with all the growth, so Dave figures Mark is probably going to ask to raise his hourly rate, which is sort of OK—except that Mark is still his biggest cash expense each month, and he really doesn't want a bigger hit. He has prepared himself for the negotiation and hopes they can come up with a compromise.

He walks into the Moose and immediately sees Mark sitting at a table with two cold beers—nice to work with people who understand the priorities. He seats himself across from Mark, and Mark gives him one of the beers and offers a toast.

"I just want to let you know how much fun it has been for me to watch the company take off and feel that I've been a part."

"Well, I sure appreciate everything you've done; it sure would have been tough without you. So did you just invite me here to buy me a beer?" Dave replies.

"Mostly that, but I also wanted to talk some business with you."

"OK, fire away, man; we've never had a lot of secrets."

"So the past few days I've been thinking about how much time I've been putting in lately with all the growth, and I thought we should talk about compensation," Mark begins.

"So I'm guessing this means you want to raise your hourly rate? You know how strapped we are for cash, but I'm willing to see if we can work something out."

"Actually, Dave, I wanted to talk to you about something a little different. You know I've been giving you guys a special deal and working late hours."

"Yeah, but remember, you chose the hours so that you weren't taking away from your regular customers, so that's kind of your choice."

"I guess it depends on how you look at it. The big thing is that I was looking at how many hours I've billed you for and the difference in rates, and I figure working for you over the past year has cost me close to ten thousand dollars, and I think we need to try to square that up, now that you're making money and all."

"Look, Mark, I hear what you're saying, but that was the deal we made; and besides, you know we barely have the cash to pay our current bills, much less pay you ten grand that we weren't expecting,. If you were planning to bill me for the difference, you should have told me from the get-go. I'm not feeling too good about this."

"No, no, no. I don't expect you to pay me the extra, but I do have a solution that I think works great for both of us without costing you any cash."

"I'm listening."

"Well, I figure that I made an investment in the company when I agreed to the reduced rate, and I've stuck by that commitment even though it's cost me money."

"And…?"

"And I'm thinking that the fair thing to do is for me to forget about the ten grand and continue to give you the hundred-dollar rate in exchange for some equity. After all, I've really invested ten grand in value and spent a ton of hours building our company, so I think it's a reasonable offer."

"Mark, I have no idea where this is coming from—you've never mentioned anything about getting paid more or equity or anything like this. And besides, weren't you the one a year ago who told me what a terrible idea it was for you to take equity in the company, since it could destroy our friendship? What's changed now?"

"Well, back then I didn't think it was a good idea, because I didn't want to burden our friendship with being partners. Now that you've got things moving along pretty well, I think we could work together without it causing any problems."

"So just so I'm clear, when I was the one with all the risk, and the equity wasn't worth a bucket of warm spit, it was a bad idea to be partners, but now that things are moving along nicely and the risk is lower, you suddenly think it's a great idea?"

"I wouldn't put it that way, but—"

"OK, let's cut to the chase, 'cause right now I'm getting more than a little pissed off. Even if I thought this was a good idea (and I don't), you know that Ed and Rick own most of the shares, and I couldn't commit to this even if I was sold on it."

"I know that, but I've spent some time with both of them, and they think you're doing a hell of a job; and I'm sure if you buy in, they'll follow your lead."

"I'm not ready to buy in, but just for the sake of argument how much did you have in mind?"

"Looking at what a ten-grand investment was worth at the start, which is when I bought in, I figure ten percent for the time I've already spend plus another five percent for keeping my fee at one hundred dollars for the next year,"

"You've got to be joking! You told me last week that you thought with all the growth we had and our IP, we could get at least a million bucks today and probably closer to two. And if we hit our five-year plan, it would be worth ten million by then, so you're saying you should get equity worth one hundred and fifty to two hundred grand today and a million five in four years?"

"I think that sounds fair, given all the time I've spent and the money I've lost to help you out."

"The only thing I think is that I need something a lot stronger than beer." And Dave walks out the door.

Two weeks later Dave had acquired a new accountant and a reputation at the golf club for being a greedy, ungrateful bastard who was happy to take help when he needed it but would stick a knife in your back when things started going well and there was money on the table.

11

OPERATIONS

I apologize in advance to those of you who have built wildly success-ful careers in some aspect of operations, but I think it's boring as hell and will readily admit it is not my strong suit. For those who are not familiar with operations, in a large company, operations can cover a very wide range of activities but for most small companies operations is really about production and some ancillary activities surrounding production (like purchasing, shipping, QC, etc.). I suspect the reason I've never had much interest in operations is because what I love about being an entrepreneur is dreaming up cool things, watching them get designed, and selling them; and the prospect of spending hours and hours figuring out how to cut production costs by a couple of points is like watching paint dry. I know it's very important and that the people who do these jobs are critical to the success of the company, and I certainly don't want to downplay the work they do; it's just not for me.

Now that I've got you all stoked about learning about operations, let's take a look at a few of the areas where you need to be involved. Now, if you happen to be one of those folks who find ops fascinating, good for you—and you are excused because if you know this stuff, I'm probably not going to teach you anything (unlike the rest of the book where every word is gospel and nothing should be overlooked). Seriously, though, even if you are fascinated with production and operations, you need to remember that your job is not production manager or COO but rather capo di tut di capo (boss of all bosses, for those not versed in mob movies), and you need to be careful to limit your role to what is needed to make things work.

As I said before, operations is mostly about manufacturing; and in my view, there is one critical role that the founder needs to have: determining how vertically integrated you want your manufacturing to be (note here that I am referring to manufacturing in the traditional sense, so if you are doing a social media start-up, that is a whole different deal). If you are going to be building a product, your options for integration range from doing everything from soup to nuts in-house to contracting out your manufacturing all the way to packaging and shipping or anything in between. There is no right answer, and I have seen companies be successful using both extremes and everything in between. So how do you decide what's right for you? Here are a few things to keep in mind:

- **Where is your value added in the product?** This is the most important question to answer for the CEO as it will not only guide operations but also help you in resource management on an ongoing basis. Let me give you a couple of examples to show what I mean. My first company made relatively inexpensive products in high volumes, so saving even a small percentage in production costs was crucial; so we made everything in-house. We brought in circuit boards and added all of the components ourselves, which allowed us to eliminate the markup of a contract manufacturer. My last company made relatively expensive products in lower volume, and the real place we added value was the software loaded on the hardware; so the hardware cost was relatively unimportant to the overall profitability of the company. It made more sense to me to put our investment into the software side of things and simply farm out the manufacturing to a contract manufacturer. Both companies produced similar results in terms of revenue, gross profit, net income, and company value, so it's just a matter of your particular product and where the value is added in the process.

- **Technical demands.** Many products today pack enormous capabilities into very small products. To accomplish this, the electronic components come in smaller and smaller footprints with correspondingly smaller connections that require complex assembly equipment and skills. Unless you are willing to invest a great deal of money in assembly technology, you may do better to work with a contract manufacturer who can spread the cost of this equipment among several customers—and don't forget that the manufacturer also assumes the risk of obsolescence of the equipment, so you don't have the risk of having to reinvest in new technology every few years.

- **Specialized components.** As noted above, contract houses can bring advantages because they install similar complex components (like microprocessors) for a number of clients, but if your product has highly specialized components the cost advantages of using a contract manufacturer are less since they can no longer benefit from volume purchasing and similar setup of assembly equipment. For example, if you have a very small product that requires Wi-Fi but with limited physical space, you may need to have a specialized chip and antenna made to your specifications, and you may do just as well to do this yourself.

- **Growth plans.** You know that you have big growth plans, and as you begin to realize this growth, your operations strategy may change dramatically; and you need to make this a key part of your annual review and planning and make adjustments as circumstances dictate.

- **Intellectual property.** You may have a product where either the design or use may require you to build in-house. If you make products for defense or other high-security applications, you may find that you have no choice but to do it all yourself. If so, remember to factor this into your price.

- **Regulatory.** In addition to the usual suspects like CE, UL, FCC, and others in the alphabet soup, there are independent organizations (notably ISO) that provide certification to manufacturing facilities that conform to standards for process and documentation. These are especially important to larger customers with international presence, and even if you can build your products cheaper, the cost of compliance with ISO may dictate that you use an ISO shop.

- **Hybrid builds.** Build-your-own or contract are not either/or choices. If your product has multiple options that require different components but also have a lot of parts in common, you might consider using a contract shop to build boards with the common components (called subassemblies) and add the custom parts in your own facility.

As with everything else we've talked about, you need to customize your manufacturing plan to meet your needs and stay as flexible as possible to accommodate changes as the company grows and technology changes. Now let's move our attention to some useful (and not so useful) measures commonly used in operations.

Quality

I've talked a lot about quality throughout the book, and here is no exception—getting high-quality products into your customers' hands is absolutely vital for the ultimate success of your company. As the saying goes, you only get one chance to make a first impression; and a product that looks or feels cheap or fails to work is a virtual guarantee that you won't be getting repeat business (and unless you're running a funeral home, repeat business is absolutely vital to your survival). Everything that impacts your customer from product quality to marketing materials to tech support to your website—it all needs to be right and of very high quality. If you see a theme developing here, it is that your primary quality focus needs to be on the customer side of the equation. People who make a fortune writing books and consulting on operations are probably already cringing in anticipation of what I'm going to say next, but here it goes: you can have a much higher tolerance for less-than-perfect quality inside the company than you can for customer-facing issues. Let me save you the angry e-mails and tweets about how you can't have quality on the outside without quality on the inside, you can't send a mixed message, people will start to cut corners everywhere, blah blah blah. Small companies are different, and sometimes getting product out the door requires doing whatever is necessary. Heresy, I know; and there is little doubt that I will burn in operations hell for saying it—but there you are.

Here's my real complaint about a lot of operational quality issues: they aren't really quality issues at all, but we call them that because in theory no one can argue about the importance of quality, so it goes unchallenged. One of my personal favorites is "first pass quality," which is basically a measure of how many just-completed products pass testing on the first try. This must be a quality issue, right? It even has quality in the title of the report, but here's the thing: FPQ (as we insiders call it) isn't a quality issue at all but rather a measure of efficiency. The point of improving FPQ yields isn't to improve quality but rather to minimize the number of products that have to be reworked, which costs extra time and money; so it's really about saving money, not quality. My point isn't that you don't want all your products to pass on the first try (of course you do, all things being equal) but that sometimes you can't afford to get distracted from what is really important. If you've got an order for five units that has to go out today for a big customer, that is what matters, even if you have to build ten units to get there. As a small business owner, is it more important to you to drop everything and fix your first pass problem or get the units out the door and keep the customer happy?

Purchasing

Welcome to the worst job in your company (other than yours, of course). Why is purchasing the worst job in the company? Simply put, it touches a lot of disciplines, and no one wants to own it. Buying parts has a technical side (engineering), a financial side (accounting), and a data entry side (whoever draws the short straw); and the worst part is that it involves a tremendous amount of back-and-forth. Engineering provides the specs for a particular part and turns it over to accounting to buy, but when the bookkeeper calls to order the part, the supplier says it is not available and suggests a replacement part. Of course, the bookkeeper has no idea if this is acceptable or not, so he or she goes back to the engineer, who, needless to say, is annoyed to have to deal with this because he or she not only has to review the product but also generate an ECN (engineering change notice) to note that the replacement part is acceptable as a build option. The engineer also privately feels that the bookkeeper did not work hard enough to find alternate suppliers, and the bookkeeper privately feels that the engineer should have made sure that the part was available before specifying it; so you also have a looming HR issue as well.

My simple rule of purchasing in the early days of your company? Don't run out of stuff.

Staffing

This is a great place to use temporary agencies. The employees you get have all the same advantages we discussed in accounting and also show up trained (theoretically). You may have to do some culling to get what you want, but using temps gives you flexibility to meet your changing needs very quickly and lets you figure out who will fit and who won't. One other thing: make sure that you keep an eye on your temps and spend time with them. On several occasions I have found relatively young people who were working temp jobs because it was relativity quick and easy to get work, but they turned out to be folks with some good education and the capability to take on a lot more. I actually found two production managers from the temp pool over the years.

I'm bored, you're bored, so let's shift gears and check in on Dave. He dealt with his production using a contract manufacturer to build subassemblies for the first four years, and it worked great, but now he is in year five, and his production manager Phil had been bugging him to bring in some equipment and build their own boards. They had done almost $2 million in revenue last year and were looking at close to $4 million next year, and he really couldn't argue that the numbers were pretty close. Still, the equipment was going to cost close to 150 grand plus another 80 or so to hire a trained operator, so Dave had managed to put him off so far. He and Phil met every morning for a few minutes to discuss priorities; and Phil arrived right at eight thirty, looking like the cat who swallowed the canary.

"Phil, I gotta tell ya, I hate to see you come in with that look on your face because I know it's going to cost me money," Dave said.

"Dave, I have to tell you, that hurts me," Phil protested. "You know I'm only looking out for your best interests every waking moment."

"Right, and I never stare at attractive women when my wife isn't around. How much do you need, and how long can I take to pay for it?"

"That's your problem, among others—you always look at the cost side of things without looking at the benefits. And besides, you're the one who always tells me to 'think outside the box'—so if some of my ideas didn't work out, it's really your fault."

"Is Maggie giving lessons now?" asked Dave. "I gotta tell you, I hear the same logic every time I come home and find some overpriced piece of 'art' in my living room. Last week it was a squirrel made out of kitchen utensils, and somehow it turned out that we bought it because I said our house was too boring, so it was my fault."

"Yeah, well, you don't pay me enough for marriage counseling, so let's get back to business," said Phil. "I've got something I think you're going to like. You remember Devaney Electronics, the contract manufacturer I worked at before I started here?"

"Yeah, good guys, as I recall."

"They are, and I stay in touch with them. Last night I had a beer with Jim, the guy who runs their production floor, and we got to talking about how we were thinking about getting our own pick and place machine but it was just too expensive. Jim told me that they had bought an ES-5500 a couple of months ago to handle the fine pitch parts they have for the BGA assembly they are doing. They had held on to the twenty-five hundred till they were sure they had all the kinks out of the fifty-five hundred, and they are thinking about selling the twenty-five hundred. Anyway, it's more than enough to handle what we need."

"Sounds good so far. How much?"

"He tells me it's worth sixty grand, and that's probably not far off, but he will sell it to me for fifty," Phil told him.

"Is it in good shape?" Dave asked.

"He says yes, and I know it worked fine a couple of years ago, but I'd budget another five or ten and do an overhaul before we put it in service. If we do it, we'll need the time to get the reels of component parts in and do the programming anyway."

"OK, but you've been telling me all along that no matter what we do for hardware, we will have to hire somebody who's factory trained, and that will cost us at least one hundred grand a year; so we're still right on the edge. And where do we find somebody to do the rebuild? That isn't gonna be cheap."

"Way ahead of you, boss. You met Lloyd, right?"

"You mean the hippie?" asked Dave.

"I mean Lloyd, the temp employee we have on board. And by the way I feel obliged to point out that using that sort of stereotype is inappropriate in today's world, and you shouldn't…"

"Shut up and get to the point."

"We seem a little sensitive this morning. OK, so I happened to mention to Lloyd about the PnP machine we were looking at, and he told me that he is a factory-certified twenty-five hundred operator," said Phil.

"No way."

"Yes way, and even better, he is actually a factory-trained technician who is fully qualified to do the teardown and retrofit if we buy it."

"So you're telling me that we have a factory-certified technician and operator who could be making one hundred grand a year who's working as a temp for us at twenty bucks an hour?"

"Nineteen fifty, actually."

"Whatever; what's the catch?" asked Dave.

"Well, it turns out Lloyd was working for a big company in LA and had a little nose candy problem," said Phil.

"No such thing as a 'little' nose candy problem, but where are we going with this?"

"I'll put it right out there—he got busted and did some time, which of course made him toxic to any big company, and he got canned. He moved up here to be around his in-laws, and the temp agency was his only option."

"So to summarize your proposal: you want to spend sixty thousand dollars of my money on a piece of used gear that you haven't seen and hand it over to a druggie with a prison record."

"I'll admit it doesn't sound so great when you put it that way, but I like this guy, and I think it's a great way to get in the game at a fraction of what it would cost normally. By my calculations, we're looking at an eight-month payback."

"How soon do you need answer?" asked Dave.

"Now would be good, or they will put the machine on eBay, but I'm sure I can stall them till noon or so," said Phil.

"Seriously?"

"Yeah, sorry, but I just found out about this."

"You really solid on this?"

"Yep."

"All right, make the deal for forty-five grand, and let's get going."

"Cool, I'm on it."

That night Dave went home, headed straight for the bar, and poured himself a double Glenlivet, which was Maggie's first clue that he was stressed.

"Tough day, hon?" she asked.

"Sort of. I'm just wondering if I really screwed up today." He went on to relate his discussion with Phil and the snap decision he'd made to spend all of their available capital—and some more that he would have to find.

"Dave, we've talked about this before. The company is doing great, and you have to get over the fact that you're getting bigger, and so are the dollars you have to spend."

"I know, but this an all-cash deal, and it's bet the company again."

"You know I hate to hear you say that. It sounds so dramatic," she told him.

"It's reality," he replied. "There are some things and decisions that are really important. If I could fund this thing by borrowing money, it would be cool, but this is literally every dime we have of free cash; and if this goes bad, we may not survive."

"You know what, just stop for a minute. You keep telling me how much different it is to sit in 'the big chair' and how you have to accept that decisions you make get done, right? So this is one of the times when you followed your instincts and made a decision, so get over it. Do you trust this guy?"

"Well, I trust Phil; and I talked to Lloyd, and he seems like a standup guy, so yeah."

"Good, so finish your scotch, and then we can go talk to *your* oldest daughter about why she super-glued her boyfriend's locker shut today," said Maggie.

"Why in the hell did she...wait, boyfriend?" Dave exclaimed.

"Yeah, believe it or not, life goes on while you're spending twelve hours a day at work. Don't worry about it, I've got it handled, but you need to be there for backup—and for god's sake, don't freak out about the boyfriend thing."

"How can I not freak out about…"

"You deal with bet the company, and I deal with bet the family. Just follow my lead."

Two weeks went by, and then a truck showed up with a very large piece of machinery along with several boxes of bubble-wrapped bits and pieces. Dave started to panic when Rick made an unexpected Friday afternoon appearance, as he hadn't really told the Hackmans about his recent purchase. Rick broke the ice. "What's up, Dave? Stuff coming in?"

"Yeah, it's our new pick and place for production. I told you about it a while back. Very cool—we're going to start stuffing our own boards and save a bunch of money."

This was a real stretch for the engineer in Dave. He had kind of mentioned the possibility of buying some used manufacturing equipment over lunch with Rick and Ed but hadn't really provided details or told them that he had already purchased it. He braced himself for one of Rick's explosions and hoped he could contain it or get him to some place where the employees wouldn't hear it.

"Oh yeah, cool. You seen my camo jacket?"

"What?"

"My camo jacket—I'm going hunting with some of my buddies, and I think I left my jacket here the other day. Never mind, I'll find it. Have a good weekend."

Dave had no idea whether to be thrilled or disgusted, so he went with thrilled.

A week later, Dave came to work in the morning to discover all his hard-earned cash flow sitting in pieces on the factory floor with no one working on it. He caught up with Phil and asked how things were going.

"Well, it's kind of weird," Phil said. "Lloyd has been great, busting his butt and working all kinds of hours to get this thing torn down, and he told me last night that it's all done and he would start putting it back together this morning."

"Sounds good."

"Yeah, except he hasn't shown up, and I can't reach him, and that's not like him."

"Shit. Well, keep me posted."

"Got it."

Two more (sleepless) days went by, and Phil showed up in Dave's office doorway around ten thirty.

"The look on your face tells me what I need to know, so give me the news," said Dave.

"Well, I finally got a call back from the temp agency, and all she told me was that Lloyd was no longer employed there. I asked why, and she told me that she couldn't say any more, just that he was no longer employed by them. I told her that we had to know what was going on and after some more time she told me that all she could say was that he violated parole."

"Parole?" exclaimed Dave.

"Yeah, news to me, too. Anyway I got her to give me the name of the parole officer and I called her, but she said she couldn't give me any info without Lloyd's permission. I finally got ahold of Lloyd, and he's coming in this afternoon at two."

When Lloyd showed up, Dave and Phil met with him in the conference room, and he was very apologetic for putting them in a bind and explained what had happened. "Here's the deal. I was over at my mother-in-law's place with my kids, watching *Cars*—my kid loves that movie—and all of the sudden the cops bust in and find a handgun on the table behind the sofa where I was with my kids. Next thing I know, I'm in cuffs, and they're hauling me off, telling me that I'm charged with being a felon in possession of a weapon. I found out later that my mom-in-law got busted for selling dope, and she rolled on me by putting the gun near me as part of the deal she cut with the cops. I was totally set up, guys."

Dave couldn't help but feel that he was having sunshine blown up his pant leg, but he was getting a little desperate given that all his free cash was sitting in parts on his factory floor, so he decided to follow up on the story.

"How long will this take to straighten out?" he asked.

"Hard to say, but I'm guessing a few months," said Lloyd.

"And till that happens, the temp agency won't employ you, right?"

"I guess."

"OK, look. I'm kind of stuck here, so what if we employ you directly as a temporary employee and see how it goes."

Phil interjected, "Dave, we need to think about this before you make this call."

"Yeah, you're right, we need to check things out. Lloyd, you OK with us talking to your PO to make sure everything's on the up and up?"

"Sure, I'll give her a call."

Dave had kept Maggie up to date on what had happened as things progressed, and she knew about the meeting and that he was following up; so she was a little anxious when he came home—even more anxious when his first stop was the liquor cabinet.

"Um, so how did your call go?" she asked.

"Well, I called the PO, and she told me that she had not heard from Lloyd and couldn't talk to me without his permission. I told her that I understood, but I explained my situation and asked if I could tell her the story he had told me, and if she could just confirm it, I could hire him."

"And?"

"And she was actually really cool about it and told me that would probably be OK, so I told her the story; and her laughter told me pretty much what I needed to know. So I said, 'I'm guessing this story isn't exactly accurate,' and her response was, 'Well, some parts are true.' 'Which parts?' I asked, and she said that she couldn't give me details, but if I replace mother-in-law's house with convenience store, I would be on the right track; and I thanked her for her time."

"So we're totally screwed?"

"Not exactly," said Dave. "Phil kind of saw this coming and found a couple of guys who were willing to work after hours and put it back together. Going to cost a small fortune, but they should have it done next week, and Phil found a guy from Devaney we can hire for a couple of months till we can get back on track."

"So it's fixed?"

"Fixed, but expensive. We can't do the kitchen remodel for a while."

"OK, I can live with that—just do what you have to do."

12

ENDGAME

Whether you are just contemplating a start-up or are right in the middle of running your own business, you have no doubt experienced far more moments of sheer terror and frustration than you have of elation and optimism, and it may seem cruel at this point to talk about executing your exit strategy. Regardless of what your exit strategy may be or how far off in the future, the key is to make sure that you go out on your terms and timing. You don't want to be forced to sell or take on partners or find yourself having to stay around years longer than you wanted because you didn't prepare your company to sell. There are a couple of important reasons for having your endgame in your sights before you even get started:

1. **Dreams and goals.** Being an entrepreneur is all about dreaming, seeing needs in the market that others don't, and building products and services to meet those needs; so why should your goals for exit be any different? You may have seen the poster that shows a guy in waders standing hip-deep in water and the caption that says, "If you are up to your ass in alligators, it's hard to remember that you came to drain the swamp." Any start-up founder understands this feeling. When you're on the phone with a supplier explaining why he hasn't been paid or dealing with another delay in the release of your big new product, it can sometimes be helpful to just sit back and remind yourself how great it's going to be.

2. **Business planning and execution.** Any time you are contemplating major decisions on strategy or investments, your exit strategy should be a factor in your planning. For example, let's assume that your exit strategy is to grow the business to a large enough volume and put it out for the highest bidder among the big players in your industry (great plan, by the way). One of the big players approaches you about a joint venture to develop a product and market it, which sounds like a great idea, and the financial aspects make it very attractive; but having this close of a relationship to one of your potential buyers may cause the others to shy away and limit the number of players when you are ready to sell. If your plan is to be the next social media giant, in order to do your IPO and become a gazillionaire, you will almost certainly need to bring in millions in VC money to get the traction in the market you need, so other funding options are probably off the table.

Does this mean that, once you set your initial exit plan, you are now locked in, and this can't change? Absolutely not. Unless you are better at this than me (or most other people I know), you are going to be years down the road before the dream starts to become a real possibility; and in that time, your situation and goals may change, or external forces like the financial markets may cause you to change your plan. Even if your overall goal (e.g., selling the company) remains the same, the path you take to get there may be very different from when you started.

Before we get too far in to this, let's review some of the options available to the small business owner who wants to get out:

- **No exit strategy.** People in this category include some I know whose job forms most of who they are. They keep putting off thinking about this as they can't imagine not working. I consider this the "die at your desk" strategy, and I really don't recommend it. Even if you have no plans or desire to retire, consider the impact your lack of planning may have on your heirs.

- **Selling out to your family.** This is kind of the "feel good" plan where you get out and get some money, and your kids get to take over a successful company. All they have to do is not screw it up, and they will get rich. Before you decide on this option, I strongly suggest that you consider the downside: what if the kids take on a bunch of debt to buy you out, and the company tanks? This could happen because the market changes or because you are a bigger part of the company's success than you care to admit. Either way, if this thing blows up, you have to be prepared for some very uncomfortable family reunions down the road.

- **Selling out to your employees.** Employee stock ownership plans (ESOPs) are another "feel good" plan where the benevolent owner sells out to his employees, and it does sound very attractive. ESOPs carry all the risks of selling out to your family plus some additional complications: they take time (usually years), and you and your employees will have to work through complicated relationship issues as ownership is transferred from you them over time. Employees become owners and eventually work to owning the whole thing, so how you manage that transition can be very challenging.

- **Initial Public Offering (IPO).** This is the stuff of legend, and if you only read the headlines of the business section, you may think that this is the main option for selling the company. In fact, however, IPOs are only a tiny fraction of the company sales today. The biggest things to keep in mind are:

  o **You have to stay around**—unlike with a stock or asset sale to another company, you will be hanging around for quite a while, so it's really fair to call this a liquidity event rather than an exit strategy. If your lifelong dream is to run a multibillion dollar company, this is perfect.

- o **You have new bosses**—you now have to answer to investors, analysts, and a whole bunch of other folks who own your company.
- o **Short-term focus**—like it or not, you will be judged by how the company performs on a quarter-by-quarter basis. This can be difficult for owners who are used to not answering to anyone.
- o **Lifestyles of the rich and famous**—get ready to have your life play out on the pages of Fortune and People. If that sounds good to you, then go right ahead.

- **Selling to a third party.** This is by far the most common method of selling ownership of a company, whether it is to an individual or another company. This is where we will spend most of our time in this section as there are better resources for the other options we've identified.

One key thing to remember when you are ready to get started: no matter what path you choose, you have just added another full-time job to the one you already have. Selling a company takes a huge amount of work; and most of the burden will fall on you, particularly if you are not advertising that the company is for sale—and this is usually the case. You generally want to keep any potential sale confidential for as long as possible because it could have negative external effects when competitors get wind of it and use that against you and negative internal effects when your employees start getting nervous over their futures with the company.

Before we get into the nitty-gritty of selling your company, let's introduce some terms that may not be familiar to most people that we will use in our sales discussion:

- **Earnings multiples:** We've touched on this before, but this is the most common method of determining the value of a company (annual net income x earnings multiple = company value). It is the equivalent of the price/earnings (P/E) ratio for publicly traded companies.

- **Mergers and acquisitions (M&A) firms:** These are companies that specialize in assisting buyers and sellers in getting together and completing a deal. They may be hired by a buyer looking for an acquisition or by sellers looking for buyers.
- **The Book:** This is a document that describes the company, markets, operations, and financial performance and is given to prospective buyers.
- **Earn-outs:** Basically, this is part of an acquisition where some of the payment is earned by the sellers after acquisition, based on the performance of the company.
- **Escrow:** The part of the purchase price that is held by a third party for a period of time after the sale to cover unforeseen issues such as product recalls.
- **Offer letter:** This is a nonbinding offer from the buyer to the seller. It outlines the proposed price and terms of purchase.
- **Due diligence:** The process by which a buyer examines the financials and operations of the company prior to completing the purchase.
- **Exclusivity:** An agreement between buyer and seller that allows the buyer a certain period of time to explore the transaction without the buyer looking for other sellers.
- **Purchase and sales agreement (PSA):** The contract between buyer and seller that defines all the terms of the sale.
- **Terms:** How and when the purchase price is to be paid (cash, stock).
- **Majority shareholder:** The person who holds over 50 percent of the shares.
- **Minority shareholder:** Everybody else.

Mergers and Acquisitions (M&A) Firms

This is probably a good time to talk a little bit about M&A firms and the value and costs that they bring. An M&A firm is a company that assists you in marketing and selling your firm in exchange for a percentage of the sales price. Most sellers use an M&A firm unless they have experience at selling a company as the process can be intimidating. I used one for my first company but handled the second one myself. The key advantages that these firms bring to the table include:

- Knowledge of the market: One of the main things you want to ask a firm you are interviewing is what experience they have in your industry. Have they done deals like yours in the past (same size and market, etc.)?
- Rolodex: For those of you who have grown up in the digital age, this is a contact list that people used to keep on a rotary file. M&A firms may have contacts in potential buyers' companies that will get you access that you might not get on your own. Most of the people have worked in the industry before going out on their own.
- Experience: They've done this before and can help you tailor the Book and the marketing materials to specific buyers.
- Negotiating skills: It's one thing to negotiate a pricing deal with one of your customers for a large purchase, but negotiating a deal that can put millions of dollars in your own pocket isn't something most of us do every day, and a little support can be helpful.
- Firewall: Odds are that at least some of the potential buyers you will be working with will either be customers or competitors. Negotiations over millions of dollars can be a little tense, as you might imagine; and you don't want to damage a relationship with a customer, so the M&A company can be a good buffer. If you are looking at a competitor as a buyer, it can be very nice to have someone who knows what you do and do not need to disclose.

So an M&A firm is a no-brainer, right? Probably, unless you have some experience at doing this and already know who your potential buyers are. You've spent years building your company to the point of selling, and you don't want to screw it up or leave money on the table out of ignorance. There are some issues to keep in mind when deciding whether to use an M&A firm or not:

- Cost: Using a firm will cost a fair amount of money. On a $25 million deal, you can expect to pay several hundred thousand dollars; you not only pay a success fee but also expenses. Just about every firm uses a model called the double Lehman scale where the firm gets 5 percent of the first million, 4 percent of the second, and so on till you get to $4 million, at which point the rest is at 1 percent per million. So you can pretty quickly figure what you will have to pay based on the value you expect to get.

- Differing interests: You have (or should have) a pretty good idea of the minimum selling price you want from the company, keeping in mind that you are going to lose about 20 to 25 percent off the top for taxes. Yes, if you want to clear $10 million on your 70 percent of the company, you will have to sell it for more than $20 million total (remember that you have to pay the M&A fee along with legal fees, which can be $50,000 or more). Whenever I was thinking about the selling price and my share, I always did a mental calculation of net, not gross. So you know what you want out of it, but what happens if a buyer gets somewhere close to what you are looking for but not quite? You need $20 million, but you have a cash buyer at $17 million who won't budge. You've spent a lot of time and money to get this close, and $17 million is a lot of money. By this point your adviser may be pushing hard for you to take the deal as he or she wants to get paid; but if you take the deal at $17 million, you will gross around $11 million and net about $8.5 million, so you are giving up $1.5 million!

- Building the Book: The good news about M&A firms is that they know the format, layout, and information the Book should have. The bad news is that the actual information, which constitutes 90 percent of what goes into the book, is info you have to provide; so you will put far more work into it than they do. Once you understand the form the Book needs to be in, the firm adds little value to the process.

- Legal fees: M &A firms are not lawyers, so you will still need to employ an attorney (and pay your accountant for the extra work). The adviser can help in these areas but can't handle the whole deal.

Whether you choose to employ an M&A firm is largely a decision you have to make on your own. I've employed an M&A firm and done my own, both with good success; and if you have concerns about the process (and you should), using an advisory firm can be money well spent. For the remainder of this discussion, I will discuss the differences between doing it yourself and using an adviser.

Let's take a closer look at each of these steps and talk about some of the options and approaches.

1. Determine the value of your company
2. Develop a list of potential buyers
3. Build the Book and send it out
4. Preliminary discussions with interested parties
5. Negotiations and offer letters
6. Due diligence
7. Develop the PSA
8. Closing
9. Wire transfer

Determine the Value of Your Company

OK, here's where it starts to get real up in here. You've watched your company's revenue and profits grow over the years, and be honest—you've kind of been thinking about what the value might be. The key thing, of course, is the earnings multiple; so how do you figure out what the right number is? There are several different options to figure out what typical multiples are in your industry: research papers, conversations with others in the industry, or M&A firms. Most industries have some sort of trade journal that tracks M&A activity. In my case, there were quarterly reports you could get for free on sales activity, multiples, and mergers. The drawback was that the figures were for the energy industry in general, and many of the transactions had nothing to do with what we were doing; so most of the industry averages were of no use to us. The good news was that they did list transactions that were similar to my company, and they provided enough information to know that typical multiples were in the eight to twelve range; so a company with $1 million in net income for the prior year could expect to receive somewhere between $8 million and $12 million gross.

This is where things start to get interesting. A 50 percent delta (difference in value) is a lot and could be the difference between whether you decide to sell or not. If the low-end number is enough, then you can go ahead; but if you need something in the middle or near the top of your expected value, you have some serious thinking to do in deciding whether you want to make the huge investment of time and effort on the process without being assured that you will get enough. There are several factors to consider. First, is your company growing rapidly? If so, you might be able to get a buyer to pay you for some of the growth you expect this year. Second, are your products better than those of the other companies that have sold for low multiples? Be very careful here; you can fool yourself, so you have to be as objective as possible. Third, do your products provide a value add for certain buyers that might lead them to pay a higher multiple? This could raise the price, but it might also narrow your list of potential buyers.

This is where an adviser may be helpful. He or she likely has more information on the sales and can help you figure where your multiple might fall on the list and also help you narrow your list of buyers. Tough call, but this is what you pay the big bucks for.

Develop a List of Potential Buyers

Before you launch into building this list, there are a few things to consider. The first thing to think about is what kind of buyer you want. Are you concerned with how a potential buyer will treat you and your employees, or do you want to receive maximum dollars and let somebody else worry about what happens next? Do you want to sell to someone you know, or are you willing to sell to a company you have no experience with? The usual answer is to maximize the selling price until you have experience working with a buyer who has very different values than you, which can lead to a very long contract post sale. There are basically two kinds of buyers: financial buyers, who are looking for a direct ROI, and strategic buyers, who not only look at ROI but also at the additional value that having your products gives them in the market. Let's look at some of your potential buyers and the pros and cons of each.

- **Customers:** People who buy your products to incorporate into their systems are a very target-rich environment. If they buy your company, they are able to get products they need without paying a markup. The advantage to you is that they may pay a higher price as a strategic buyer than as a financial buyer. The downsides are that you will be revealing your financials to a customer (and if for some reason the deal falls through, you may have info in the market that you don't want out there) and that if there are tensions in the negotiations, you could damage a relationship.
- **Competitors:** Once again, this is a strategic buyer group with a very high potential for giving you a better price. Keep in mind, however, that you are exposing a lot of information about your company, not just financials but also strategic plans and new products in the pipeline. Generally speaking, the larger the competitor, the lower the risk, as large companies tend to have more firewalls between their acquisitions group and operations, but you still never know.
- **Other strategic buyers:** There are some other buyers to consider, including companies that may want to get into the market

but are not players today. Companies like Google, which tend to look outside of their traditional markets and products, may be looking to get into a space where they do not currently participate, so don't rule them out completely (and many of the high-tech success stories today are sitting on boatloads of cash and might pay a premium price). Another option to consider is private equity firms that invest in specific areas and build portfolios of companies in a narrow market as they really function more like strategic buyers.

- **Financial buyers:** These are private equity firms that look to acquire companies as part of an investment portfolio but are not strategic buyers. They look at you like they would stocks, junk bonds, or Krugerrands—you are an investment, and they are looking for a return. They are usually tougher on price and are much more likely to turn around and flip the company at any point. If you are interested in either of the equity buyer pools, you may benefit from using an adviser firm—you probably know your competitors and customers, but you may not be aware of noncompetitors looking to get in the market; and you probably have no knowledge of private equity players.

Regardless of which of these groups you decide to pursue, bear in mind that broadening your net is more likely to produce a higher price but will also take up much more of your time. If you are inclined to go for a big pool, using an M&A firm can take a lot of the load off of your shoulders.

There is something else to keep in mind as you are building your business: as you get bigger and more recognized, you are likely to get calls from the acquisitions groups of your customers and competitors, asking if you are interested in selling. By the time I got done with my last company, I was getting at least one or two of these calls a month. How you handle them is very critical. You need to handle these calls diplomatically, but if you are not ready to sell, you don't want to waste their time or yours; so have a plan in mind. My strategy was to have a number in mind that was significantly more than the company was worth but enough that if someone paid it, I would be happy to leave. I could tell the buyer that I was always interested in selling, but that I needed a number that was probably too steep for them to justify and tell them what it was. The usual response was, "Wow, that is pretty steep; I don't think I could sell that to my bosses." At that point I would say that I was a little crazy and probably not ready to sell just yet but would certainly contact them as things changed and that they could feel free to stay in touch. This way they knew that I was likely willing to sell at some point, and I always made sure to add them to my list of people I would call first when the time came. You may think this acquisitions stuff is all hush-hush black ops, but in reality, it is pretty much out in the open. I sold my last company to a customer/partner who had told me that if I ever decided to sell, they were interested; when the time came, and I called, they were ready to roll.

Build the Book and Send it Out

I capitalize "the Book" because it will take on so much importance in your life that it deserves all the respect it can get. For the most part, it will be the primary early contact between you and potential buyers; and it needs to sell your company all on its own. Any prospect will spend some time reading through it but will put far more time into it if it is well put together and does a good job of making your case. The Book will likely run nearly a hundred pages by the time you are done, and nobody will take the time to read all of it if the material is difficult to follow or inconsistent. One of the biggest challenges in assembling the Book is the variety of people who will be reading it. Some may be very familiar with your company (though the acquisitions people are less likely to have a lot of knowledge) while other prospects may have very limited awareness of your industry and company. The Book needs to be thorough without having tons of info that most people already know; this is a much bigger challenge than you may think. I'm not going to go into great detail here about the Book—if you've done or seen one, you already know what it is; and if you haven't, you should definitely get some help on this, as it's far too important to just wing it. What you put in your Book may vary some, but here are most of the key components:

- Overview: This is a one- or two-page summary of the company's history, products, markets, and competitive advantage. You want it to be a little salesy, but don't overdo it. There is plenty of time to make your case, and all you really want to do with the overview is get unfamiliar buyers up to speed in a general way on who you are and where you compete. This will include some summary information about financial performance (revenue growth, margins, and net income).

- Markets: Where do you compete, who are the major competitors, and what are the characteristics of this market? Is it growing, and why? Is it domestic or international? What are the key challenges your customers face? How will this change in the future?

- Competitors: Who are your competitors, and what market share do they have? What are their strengths and weaknesses, and how do you attack them? What do they do differently than you do?

- Customers: Whom do you sell to? If you have different types of customers, break them down by type. What are their needs, and how are you solving them? What is changing in the market, and how do you plan to adapt to these changes?

- Products: This is a summary of all the products you make and the competitive advantages they have in the market. The focus here is not technical, as these are not technical buyers, but rather on features, functions, and benefits.

- Sales and marketing: How do you go to market? If your strategy and tactics are different than competitors' and provide an advantage, this is the time to highlight it. How many employees do you have, and what do you farm out to others?

- Engineering: Who are the key players of your engineering team? Is your focus on hardware or software? Does the intellectual property you have built provide you with a significant advantage? Do you have key patents?

- Operations: How do you build your products? What key quality measures do you have in place? Do you test every product before it goes out the door? Are your processes automated, or are things done by hand?

- SWOT: This stands for the strengths, weaknesses, opportunities, and threats your company faces in the markets. One note here: be very frank about your weaknesses and threats and don't try to hide them. Odds are buyers will figure them out themselves, and you end up either looking like you are covering things up or (worse) like you are unaware of them. Put them on the table and make sure to let them know how you are dealing with them, either here or in the other sections.

- Financials: You want to provide the previous five years' financial performance year by year and the trailing twelve months' financials by month. If there is anything that you want to highlight, you might want to put in bullet points as an intro (for example, five-year average annual growth of 41 percent). If there are negative areas in your reports, you can consider bringing them up to explain, but be very careful here as you may bring attention to something that they consider unimportant. The things most buyers are looking for are good, consistent growth in revenue; improved gross margin; operating expenses in line with revenue; and growth in net income.

- Five-year plan: Here is where you present your plan for the next five years. It should primarily involve financials, but you may include any significant changes you expect—new markets, significant product introductions, and so on. This is your chance to really sell them on how great things are going to be, but try to restrain yourself. If you make assumptions about the future that are very different than the past (e.g., your last five years' growth was 30 percent, but you suddenly expect it to be 50 percent), you had better be prepared to do some explaining. They are going to discount whatever you give them anyway, and the more unrealistic your assumptions, the greater the discount. Unless you really do see something wildly different, you are much better off to use historical numbers.

If this doesn't scare or intimidate you, then I've clearly done a poor job of outlining the task you have. This is probably one of the most unique and challenging projects you will ever take on—all you have to do is be brief but provide plenty of detail, be honest but encouraging, and be pragmatic but visionary. Good luck.

Now comes one of the most challenging parts of this process. After you (or your adviser) have had some preliminary discussions with potential buyers, you or they may send out a very brief summary before providing the Book to gauge interest. This brief offer summary is usually anonymous, but if you are in a relatively small industry, there are very few secrets. Anyhow, you will have pared down the number of prequalified prospects, and you will now face a big challenge: you, of course, want nondisclosure agreements (NDAs) in place, but many shoppers will either refuse or will want an NDA that is so watered down that it isn't worth much. If they are customers, you may already have an NDA in place that might cover this, but don't count on it. At some point you will likely have to accept something much weaker than what you want and simply trust people. If you feel comfortable based on discussions you've had, send them the Book and hope for the best.

Preliminary Discussions with Interested Parties

You might expect that this is the point where there is a dramatic drumroll, and you unveil the asking price—not so much. I mentioned earlier that I am a fan of getting your price out there early, and believe me, so are your potential new owners. Nobody wants to spend a bunch of time screwing around and reading the Book if your expectations are way out of line. Now it goes without saying that the price you put out there is near or slightly above the high side of the range you determined earlier (not so far out that it's laughable), and the buyer already has his or her idea of what he or she wants to pay and has told you that you are too high. This is all part of the game—you figure they will come up some, and they figure you will come down some; so as long as your numbers are within maybe 20 percent of each other, you may have reached this point if they didn't see something in the book that scared them off.

Hopefully, at this point, you have one or more interested parties who want to move forward and pursue a deal. If you do not have anyone still interested, the odds are your price is simply too high, because there is a price that your company will sell for—just not what you want. You now have a couple of options: (1) recalibrate your expectations and contact the prospects to let them know you were just kidding (awkward, to say the least, and leaves you in a very weak negotiating position); or (2) piss on the fire and call in the dogs, 'cause the hunt's over (and you just need to keep building the company till you can get what you want). But of course you've been smart and realistic, so you have some folks sniffing around.

This is the point where buyers will want to come out and visit and see you face to face and look at your operations—and this is wonderful, but it also creates some awkward moments. In all likelihood, you have kept your plans fairly quiet, and only a handful of employees know what you are contemplating, but now you are going to have teams of people coming to your building and taking tours and meeting in the conference room. If you ignored my advice earlier about hiring the best people, you may find you can pull this off with no one noticing; but assuming you have pretty bright folks hanging around your shop, they will know something is up. You may be able to hold them off for a while by telling them that your customer is interested in partnering and doing more business, but that likely won't fly if the buyer is a competitor. When do you tell them? Hell if I know—this is one you just have to play by ear and see how it goes.

Most buyers will send a team of people to visit; this is another awkward time, as you can almost bet that some of the people on this team will be operations people who work with folks on your team, and the firewall we discussed early is blown apart. You are well within your rights to insist on an NDA here—you've already exposed confidential information, and based on that information, they want to pursue it further; so it's entirely reasonable. This is where they want to meet you and key members of your team and see if there seems to be a fit between the two of you. They also want to look around and get a feel for things like your real estate, equipment, and people. If this visit goes well and they like what they see, let the games begin.

Negotiations and Offer Letter(s)

OK, here's what you've spent the last however many years getting ready for: you are going to make a deal to sell your company. Unless you have literally bargained for your life with some terrorist group, this will be the most gut-wrenching, exhausting negotiation you will face in your life. You are actually talking about millions of dollars that either will or will not show up in your checking account in a few months. Once you make the deal (unless something extraordinary happens), within a short time, you will no longer own this business that you have brought from your basement to a place where a multibillion dollar international company wants it badly enough to take it off your hands and make you rich. Cool, and a pretty big deal.

If you do not have an M&A adviser, at this point everybody but you and their point man leaves the room (literally or figuratively), and it's up to the two of you to either make a deal or not. Both of you have the authority to obligate all the others, and you will certainly keep your partners up to speed, but it's all on you and him or her. You've already put your number out there, so shut the hell up and let him or her do the talking and put the buyer's offer on the table. Once the other company's number is out there as well, you know what kind of delta you have to close; assuming that their number is at least close to the minimum, you'll accept. If they simply accept your number, ask for a break and go to the bathroom and bang your head against the wall, because you just left some money on the table (or if you have an adviser, go punch him or her in the face for giving you lousy advice). As I think there is an entire other book I plan to write on negotiations, I won't belabor the process, but please don't immediately offer to meet in the middle—it's weak, and that becomes the new highest price you can get.

I will say that this is one area where having an M&A firm can be really comforting. Not only do you have someone to advise you on negotiating strategy, you also have a buffer between you and the buyer. Offers and negotiations will go through your adviser and give you much more opportunity to hit the pause button and think about what is on the table and how you want to respond.

This will also be the time when any terms besides cash will be put on the table. If the buyer wants to pay with anything besides cash—things like stock in their company or any earn-out expectations—they need to put that on the table now. In my opinion, you should get the best cash offer you can get; simply put, you know the value of cash in your hand today, and anything else has an unknown value. Might be more, might be less, but why take the chance? Be very careful of earn-outs—they sound attractive but are very dangerous. For those not familiar with the term, earn-outs are essentially offers that are part cash today with another portion that can be earned over a period of time after sale by hitting certain financial expectations. It can be very tempting to go this route, but remember one thing about the postsale future: you are no longer in charge, they are—and they can make it impossible for you to hit the numbers that you expect. I had a friend who sold a contracting company with earn-outs and fully expected to get all the money because the numbers didn't even have to be as good as they had been for the last five years. The company leased space in an industrial park at a very low cost as it was mostly warehouse and shop, but the lease was up, and the acquirer had some Class A office space that was vacant and moved the contractor into that space. The rent quadrupled, and the higher operating expenses ate up all the company's profits. Oops. And yes, you can try to negotiate terms that will protect you, but it is very difficult to anticipate everything that can come up.

Once you agree verbally to the price and terms, the buyer will produce an offer letter that summarizes the terms you've agreed to and provides the expectations for completing the deal and getting to closing. Assuming you agree with what's in the letter, you sign; it and assuming that there are no issues uncovered in due diligence, you have sold your company.

Due Diligence

Ever had a three-month-long colonoscopy with no anesthetic? Welcome to due diligence. Before your celebratory hangover has gone away, you will receive a document from the buyer detailing the information that you will need to provide them to complete the sale, and it is a lot. At this point they have the right to ask for anything and everything, including examining your books, employee records, e-mails, leases, customer agreements, legal documents, patents, software, hardware, contracts, credit card statements, regulatory findings, and to talk with any employees about any topic. They will send accounting teams to sit in your office and go through all of the financial statements and documentation, a process usually involving three to four people in your building for two to three weeks. They will also send teams for HR, engineering and operations, and you just have to smile and take it. They will likely generate questions that you and your staff will have to answer; and if they find anything they don't like, they can either walk away from the deal or negotiate a lower price.

The physical toll of due diligence is rough enough, but it also can be very hard for you to deal with on another level. You are a privately held company, and to this point you have only had to answer to your family and the IRS for choices you have made; now suddenly you have somebody looking over your shoulder and second-guessing everything you've done. Push back too much, and you will make them wonder what you're hiding, so up to a point, you simply have to put up with it. A few months down the road, when you've been through the examinations and are on the third round of answering the same questions, you are well within your rights to call the buyer and insist on a final round of questions and a commitment to a closing date. Until then, you are not in charge.

One other note about due diligence: you may be tempted not to disclose things or point out items they have missed, but be very careful. Yes, it's their responsibility to get the information to be satisfied, but any deficiency in disclosure could result in litigation or holdbacks on your escrow funds. In one of my sales, we were within a couple of weeks of closing when I realized they had not reviewed any of our technical information—no engineering documents, software, or intellectual property. Knowing that a lot of the value they put in the company was the intellectual property, I called them and pointed this oversight out to them, and they hastily put together a team to come out and meet with our engineering team. The amount of time they spent paled in comparison to the seven man-weeks of time they spent on finance, but at least if they came back later and complained, I could point out that I was the one who raised the issue, which I have to think would be a pretty solid defense in court. Fortunately it didn't come to that, but hopefully you get the point—you want a happy buyer, so make sure you are as accommodating as possible.

Purchase and Sales Agreement (PSA)

As this is the document that legally transfers ownership of the company, you might expect that we would spend a lot of time on it, but we won't. Simply put, hire a really, really good lawyer who has a great deal of experience in this area and stay the hell out of his or her way. Read the PSA and address any questions you have to your lawyer. You have to trust your lawyer absolutely; and if you don't, get another lawyer.

Escrow

Part of the purchase price will be held by a third party to cover any costs that may come up that are the responsibility of the seller. These include any legal judgments, product recalls, patent infringement, and any known material issues that were withheld in due diligence. You want this to be as small as possible, but you can expect 20 percent or so to be in escrow for a couple of years with half released at year one anniversary and the balance two years after closing.

Closing

This is where you sign the papers (and there are a lot of papers). Once again, trust your lawyer and make sure that he or she reviews any paper you sign, no matter how unimportant it may seem.

Wire Transfer

The day the papers are signed and exchanged, the buyer sends you a wire transfer for more money than you ever dreamed of. One word of advice: buy a spare mouse for your computer as you will hit the refresh button on your online banking site so often that the left button on the mouse will be worn out. Today is a day when commas will be your favorite punctuation mark. Nice work.

Of course, our story wouldn't be complete without finding out how things wound up for our old buddy Dave Lavin. Move ahead a few years from our last visit to Dave, and he is in the office early one morning when he looks up to see Ed Hackman chatting with Kathy, the office manager.

"Hey, Ed, didn't know you were coming by today. Uh, Rick's not here right now."

"No shit—it's Friday," says Ed. "And please don't try to look shocked that I know his schedule; I think we're both way past that now."

"Ten-four," says Dave. "So to what do we owe the honor of your presence today?"

"Actually, I came to see you—got a minute?"

"Sure, let's go back to my office."

On their way to Dave's office they stop by the break room for coffee, and Ed points to the snack table full of goodies. "I see Maggie's still going to Costco every week for a snack run. You've got what, forty people now? That's gotta be getting expensive," he says.

"Actually, she makes one run on Monday, and I have to go again after work on Wednesday," says Dave. "It's not cheap, but folks love it; and at the end of the day it works out to like fifteen dollars a head, so it's really not that bad."

"And you still barbeque every month for the employee meeting?"

"If the weather's good; otherwise Maggie brings something in. But grill days are the best—the employees think I'm doing them a big favor by throwing some burgers on the grill, and I don't have the heart to tell them how nice it is to get some fresh air and a break in the day."

Settling into his chair, Dave notices that Ed has closed the door, which almost never happens around here. "Ed, if you're firing me, can we make it quick? I can still work in a tee time if you don't drag this out," he says.

"No such luck, kid. If you want to get canned, you're going to have to stop making so much money for me. You remember Joann Clark from Bindaire?"

"Sure, I know the company, but everybody calls them Bindaire Dundat. I couldn't forget that name, but I don't remember Joann."

"Do us both a favor and get the smartass remarks out of your system before you meet with her next week," says Ed.

"I didn't know I was meeting her next week."

"I took the liberty of telling her that you would have dinner with her at the trade show in Chicago."

"Thanks. Any reason in particular, or are you branching out into setting up speed dates?"

"You wish. No, she's way out of your league in every category I can think of, but she is interested in buying us."

"Come again?" says Dave.

"Oh, now I have your attention?" says Ed. "I didn't get a lot of details, but she is now in charge of acquisitions for Bindaire, and we are on her short list. Apparently they have a boatload of cash and some activist investors, and they think we might be a good fit."

"So have you told Rick yet? Is he finally going to make an appearance at a trade show and break his undefeated streak?"

"Funny, Dave. And the answers to your questions are yes and no. Yes, I told him; and no, he's not going—she specifically asked to meet with you as the first step."

"And he's OK with that?" asks Dave.

"Yeah, I explained that it's more of a technical acquisition for them, and so she wanted to talk engineering and product details with you first," says Ed.

"Seems a bit weird…she actually told you that?"

"As far as you know, yes. Anyhow, dinner's on Wednesday, and we need a good impression, so try not to eat your steak with your fingers. Oh, one other thing—you need to see if we have an NDA with them, as it would probably be useful, but I told her you would only talk about revenue and profit in broad numbers."

"So what am I supposed to tell her about selling?" asks Dave.

"I don't know; you're the president—but if it sounds good to you, I'd be up for a deal," says Ed. "I've got my eye on a fifty-one-foot Meridien yacht and could use the cash. Keep me posted."

Needless to say, Dave gets almost no sleep the entire weekend, and by Sunday morning he is driving Maggie crazy.

"Dave, I think you've pushed those eggs at least a quarter of a mile around your plate," she tells him. "Are you going to eat them or continuing doing laps? I've never seen you like this."

"Do I have to remind you how important Wednesday night is?" he says.

"No, the first ten times were enough—and that's not counting at least twice in your sleep last night."

"I've never done anything even remotely like this. I don't know what to say, who talks first, what to wear, or…"

"I can't help with the numbers or negotiating strategy, but I can help with your wardrobe—and besides, you need to get out of the house. Even the dog's avoiding you."

"You know, that's not a bad idea," he says. "In fact, when I was over at Costco getting snacks, I saw they had some brand-new Kirkland dress shirts that looked pretty sharp, and—"

"No."

"These weren't the ones you're thinking of; these are much nicer, and,—"

"No. You are not going to negotiate a deal worth millions of dollars in a fourteen-dollar shirt," Maggie says firmly.

"I told you these were nicer; I think they're almost twenty dollars, and—"

"Enough. Put on your shoes and get in the car. I'm driving."

Dave has a minor panic attack when she pulls up to Nordstrom's, and there are a couple of uncomfortable moments with the weird guy measuring his inseam, but four hours later Dave leaves $2,400 poorer with a suit, a jacket, three shirts, two ties, two pairs of pants, and a brand-new pair of shoes. Despite the sticker shock, he does at least feel that he has enough options to have things covered (though he still has no idea what is appropriate). Wednesday afternoon rolls around, and his confused explanation for leaving the show at four o'clock leaves his sales guys totally perplexed, but he wants to make sure he does it right. After spending more time in front of the mirror than his girls had for prom, he settles on the jacket, no tie, and the dressier pants, which he thinks strikes just the right balance of a little dressy but still casual enough for a start-up guy; and he heads off for dinner. He'd scouted the location of the steakhouse earlier to make sure he was going to the right place, but he's so nervous that he arrives almost a half hour early. This presents a major quandary: he can't go to the table, and he can't leave, which leaves the bar as his only option. This is a risky play—on the one hand, it shows that he is relaxed enough to have a drink, but he's been too nervous to eat all day, and one scotch might hit him hard enough that she'll think he is an out-of-control alcoholic. After one drink and two bowls of pub mix, Joann finds him in the bar, and they go to eat.

"Dave, it's great to meet you, and I apologize for the short notice," she says.

"No worries," he replies. "I have to admit, after talking with Ed, I'm a little intrigued."

"Glad to hear it. Since I asked for the meeting, let me start by telling you a little about Bindaire and why we're here. If you've followed the financial press, you know that we have accumulated a fair amount of cash—in fact, pretty close to five billion dollars. We're not Apple or Microsoft, but for our size, that's quite a lot of money. We have some activist investors who either want us to do something with it or give it back to them as a special dividend. Needless to say, our senior management is not particularly thrilled about a dividend, but we cut back our expenses so much in the recession that we can't reinvest it fast enough to stay ahead of the inbound cash flow."

"Sounds like a good problem to have."

"It is an upscale problem to have, and it beats most of the other options, but it's still a problem. Where you come in is that one of the priorities they've set for using the cash is acquisitions, particularly strategic buys that complement our existing products. The issue we've had is that we've always handled deals at the corporate level, and with all the time and work involved, they've had a minimum acquisition price of at least two hundred and fifty million."

"Sold!"

"Nice try, but we've fixed that problem. Instead of running it all through corporate, they've put a certain amount in each of the operating business units and put teams in charge of finding smaller companies that fit our specific markets. And all the CFO and his team do is sign off, as long as we stay in budget. Basically, I write the checks, but I'm using their checkbook, so they get final say. Nice part is, it shortens the process a lot, and we can turn deals that are important to us as a business unit. The reason we're here today is that I went to a meeting of our VPs and area GMs a month or so ago and asked them to each put together a list of companies that we should look at. At the risk of hurting my negotiating position, I can tell you that your company was the only one that turned up on every list, so I figured we should talk."

"That's nice to hear for sure," says Dave. "At the risk of hurting my negotiating position, I've never done anything like this, so I have no idea how it goes or even where to start."

"I hear you, and the first thing I would say is just relax and be yourself," Joann tells him. "I've been doing this for ten years now, and one of the reasons I like to meet face-to-face instead of in a conference room full of people is that I want to get a chance to know who I'm working with. If things proceed like we hope, you and I will be spending a lot of time together over the next few months, and I hope we can be pretty candid with each other. Remember, we wanted to talk to you not only because we are interested in the company but because we're interested in you. We know that you aren't the majority shareholder, but we also know that you run the show, and we want you to stay if we make a deal."

"Sounds good so far. What can I tell you?"

"Well, Ed and I discussed some ground rules, and I can understand that he doesn't want to disclose too much confidential information this early, but I certainly want to figure out tonight if we can get close enough to move on and not waste each other's time, so I have a proposition: we've done some basic research on you guys, and I think we have a pretty good feel for where you are."

"OK," says Dave.

"What I propose is that I will tell you what we think and you just tell me if we are way off base or in the ballpark," says Joann. "Hopefully we can get close enough to get some numbers on the table and see where we are."

"I'm game—certainly sounds like a good approach."

"Good! Let's start with revenue. My team has done some homework, and their best guess is that you are somewhere between seven and eight million dollars; is that in the ballpark?"

As Dave had just gone over the numbers before the meeting, and the prior twelve months' revenue was $7.6 million, he was already starting to wonder if they had a mole.

"You're pretty close."

"OK, then we're off to a good start, so let's talk net income. If we assume the midrange of seven-point-five for revenue, I'm guessing that you're throwing off around one-point-five million. Yes?"

"This is a little scary, but yeah, you're not far off." The actual number was $1.4 million, and now Dave was sure they had inside info.

"It's really not that tough when you've done as many deals as I have. You get a pretty good feel for a company's size and how well it's run—no magic, really. So we'll call it a million five. I'm sure you've thought about a number you want, so what are you thinking?"

And just like that, a nice dinner had turned into the biggest decision of his life in about twenty seconds—go too high and they walk away; too low, and you give up millions.

"Well, we've kicked it around a little bit, and I met with the accountants last week, and we think that with all the growth potential, we need to be in the twenty to twenty-five million range to go ahead."

"I'm sure it won't surprise you to hear that our numbers are more in the sixteen to eighteen range. That's a pretty big spread between our low and your high, but on the other hand, the difference between your low and our high is only about ten percent, which means if you're willing to negotiate a little, we're willing to come out and take a look and give you a chance to wow us, and we might loosen the purse strings a little bit. Based on what I've seen, I like you, and we certainly like your company, so if you're game, let's see where this goes. What do you say?"

"Works for me. What's next?" asks Dave.

"We'd like to see some additional information about the company—financials, operations, and so on," says Joann. "We have a standard format we like to use, if it's OK with you—speeds things along if we can go to the CFO with a package that looks like what he expects, and it makes everybody's lives easier. As soon as we get a chance to look at that, I'll send a team out for a quick look at the company—meet your management team, see the operations, and all that. They'll put together a report for me. If everything looks good, we can work out a final number, and I'll get you an offer letter. We do some due diligence, and I'll just apologize in advance for that; it's run by finance, and you will hate them and me by the time it's done. Try to accommodate them as much as possible, but if it really gets out of hand, give me a call, and I'll see if I can rein them in a little."

Bottom line, they ended up at $19.5 million, and Dave had a three-year contract. They wanted five years, and he wanted one year, so they sweetened the deal by five hundred grand and upped his salary by 30 percent in exchange for the three-year deal, so everybody was happy—at least until Dave and Maggie went out for their incredibly expensive celebratory dinner.

"Honey, you know I had some doubts, and I was thinking back today to when we started," says Maggie. "I am so impressed with what you've done, I almost can't believe it. Whoever thought we'd have this kind of money—we're living the American dream!"

"Yep, and in just three short years, we can do whatever we want," says Dave.

"That brings up the one subject I haven't raised: can you tolerate working with Rick for another three years without killing him?"

The wine was getting to Dave (they had a limo waiting outside), and he hadn't thought all the way through his answer. "That's the great part—Bindaire figured out who was really doing the work, and they insisted that I have a longer contract. Rick will only be around for six months. I gotta be honest; it felt pretty good to sit in the meeting with all of the management team and have Joann tell us all that, including Rick. For once the real truth was on the table."

"Um, hon? I know you negotiated the whole deal, but did you negotiate the employment contracts?"

"No, Ed suggested that we each negotiate our own contracts with Bindaire using our personal lawyers so there wasn't any conflict. Makes sense when you think about it."

"So Rick gets fifty percent more money than you, but you have to work two and a half years longer than he does?"

Dave started to point out the flaw in her logic, but then he realized that he had been so busy putting the deal together that he'd never thought of it that way.

"Son of a bitch!"

And Dave learned that even a large minority shareholder was still a minority shareholder.

If you've been on the fence about doing a start-up, and what I've said has scared you off, good for you for knowing to back away. This is a 100 percent commitment, and if you (or your spouse) aren't sold, don't do it.

Good luck, and thanks for reading.

www.ingramcontent.com/pod-product-compliance
Lightning Source LLC
Chambersburg PA
CBHW051636170526
45167CB00001B/218

* 9 7 8 1 5 0 0 1 4 6 9 8 6 *